HA
BELIE v ELAND

PHIL BARTH

PHIL BARTH

DEDICATION

To mom and dad, who took me to watch Gaylord Perry pitch against the Oakland A's.

To dad, who sat on the couch next to me and watched Greg Pruitt put some sick moves on the defenders.

To my friends Chris and Donna, who still text back and forth when we watch the games miles apart.

To my wife and children who don't understand how anyone could be so crazy about Cleveland sports, but love me anyway, and even watch the playoffs with me.

INTRODUCTION

I'm Phil Barth… and I'm a Cleveland fan.

That's not an introduction to a 12 step program, although a year ago it could have been.

Up until 2016 we were subjected to a string of heart breaks: Red Right 88. The Drive. The Fumble. The 1997 World Series.

The city of Cleveland did not win a championship for 52 years. The only other city in North America with a longer drought is San Diego (53 years). But that's mostly a two sport drought. Buffalo is at 51 years – but again – two sports.

The city of Cleveland experienced a total of 152 seasons between championships. 52 baseball (1964 to 2015), 49 football (1964 to 2015, less 3 years without a team), 45 basketball (1970 to 2015), and 6 hockey (1972-1975 WHA, 1976-1977 NHL).

And of course in the middle of our streak we had our football team taken away by a bastard named Art Modell.

Then there was that whole ESPN "Decision" special in 2010… But we've moved on from that. Forgive and forget I always say.

Throughout the drought our faith was tested. But we never gave up. (Okay, I gave up on the Cavaliers for a few years – more on that later). There's a reason why ESPN's documentary was called "Believeland". It wasn't always easy to believe that better times would come, but believe we did.

And in 2016 our belief was rewarded. The Cavs are the NBA champions. The Indians are the AL champions. The Browns… well, they won a game.

But even when times were tough, Cleveland sports gave me a way to relate to others: Friends, family, and even friends of my family.

Bill Baumler was a family friend. Bill ran a sporting goods (mostly fishing) distribution business in Lorain. He stored product in our barn. He would come up in his truck, selling to bait shops between Lorain and Marblehead. He would then re-load at our barn, and continue selling up to

Toledo. He rented a guest room, and enjoyed a good game of pinochle with my grandma, mom and dad.

Absolutely none of that was relatable to a 10-year-old kid. But Bill and I were able to talk frequently – about the Indians. I remember a conversation with him about Jim Kern. He said "Hey the Indians called up this young guy, Jim Kern." I immediately started talking about how many guys Kern struck out in Oklahoma City that year (220), and Tulsa the year before that (182). From then on we had great conversations. It didn't matter that Bill was 45 years older than me. We had Cleveland sports in common.

THE THEME OF THE BOOK:

This book recounts some of the moments that shaped Cleveland sports, and in the process shaped me. There are some bad results, to be sure. But know this: The Cavs section has a happy ending.

In the case of the games and key moments – I describe in (frequently painful) detail the key moments. I don't have an identic memory. Hopefully no Cleveland sports fan does. I have YouTube. I watched each of the games in question to remember how I felt when I watched them live.

That's right: In writing this book I actually **re-watched** Red Right 88, The Drive, The Fumble, The Shot, Game 6 of the 1995 World Series, Game 7 of the 1997 World Series and Games 5-7 of the 2007 ALCS.

That was stupid. Never again.

On the bright side, I re-watched Game 7 of the 2016 NBA finals repeatedly. And I will again, and again and again. I also watched some of the "scene setting games", like the 1986 double OT win over the Jets, Game 4 of the 1997 Divisional Playoffs (Sandy Alomar goes yard on Mariano Rivera) and Game 1 of the 1995 ALDS (Tony Pena ends it in the 12th).

My general strategy was to watch one of the sad list followed by one from the happy list, followed by another watching of Game 7 of the 2016 NBA finals.

The book is in three sections. It covers the teams chronologically:

Part One – The Cavs.
Part Two – The Indians.
Part Three – The Browns.

If you like happy endings, read it from back to front.

PART 1: THE CAVS

"Hey can I have my LeBron jersey back?" – Phil Barth to my father-in-law, July 2014.

A FAN IS BORN - THE MIRACLE OF RICHFIELD

As kids we didn't pay a lot of attention to the Cavs. Even when we played on the playground we were the Boston Celtics: Paul Silas, John Havlicek, or Dave Cowens. I got to be Hank Finkel.

Then one day one of my buddies got a red, white and blue basketball. Just like the ABA. And suddenly we didn't care about even the legendary Celtics. The ABA was the coolest. When we played we were picking names like Dr. J. George Gervin or Moses Malone. I got to be Hank Finkel.

Frankly, the Cavaliers weren't good or interesting. I never took note of them. In fact, it wasn't until 1975 that I even knew the Cavs existed. At that point my sixth grade teacher Mr. Rinaldo gave me a Cleveland Cavaliers Media guide. He was probably just trying to shut me up.

It worked. To this day I remember reading about the players:

Jim Chones, the former ABA center. The Cavaliers got his rights from the Lakers for a first round draft pick.

Bingo Smith, the small forward who could shoot the lights out, and often did.

Campy Russell, the second year forward. He was a first round pick (and a good one) from Michigan.

Jim Brewer, the tough defensive power forward.

Austin Carr, the number one pick in the 1971 NBA draft.

Dick Snyder, a guard / forward who came from Seattle in exchange for a first round draft pick swap in 1974.

Jim Cleamons, the starting point guard the Cavs stole from Los Angeles for a second round draft pick.

Foots Walker, the 6'0" tall backup point guard from West Georgia University.

I decided to check them out. The guide listed the schedule and the station. Just like the Tribe, the Cavs were broadcast on WWWE (1100 AM).

I turned on a game one evening. Joe Tait was doing the play by play. "Austin Carr… to the line to the lane to the hoop – got it!" "Bingo Smith, 22 footer…. BINGOOOO!" I was hooked.

And just in time. The Cavs were getting good.

With the pieces in place the Cavs finished 1974-75 at 40-42, tied with the Knicks for the final playoff spot. Unfortunately, the Knicks won the tiebreaker and moved on to the playoffs.

The Cavs started slowly in 1975-76. They went 8-14 in their first 22 games. But changes were coming. On November 27 the Cavs acquired center Nate Thurmond from the Chicago Bulls. There were other players involved (Rowland Garrett to the Cavs, Steve Patterson and Eric Fernsten to the Bulls), but the key was Thurmond. He was a 34-year-old center who locked down the middle. It allowed the Cavs to give much needed rest to Jim Chones. Thurmond was no longer a starter, but he was just what the Cavs needed off the bench.

I liked Thurmond. He looked older than 34, but he blocked a ton of shots and grabbed a bunch of rebounds. Even better, he liked Cleveland. He was in a TV Commercial for the Cleveland Plain Dealer. There were a bunch of people signing different parts of a Plain Dealer jingle. At one point it's Nate Thurmond, spinning a basketball on his finger. He sings "You read it every day." And on the word "day" he drops his hand, and the ball just stays there and keeps spinning. Thurmond smiles at the camera as if to say "I got you, didn't I?"

The rest of the winter I listened to Joe Tait describing the action. The Cavs kept winning. The more they won the more excitement Tait brought. The more excitement Tait brought the less sleep I got. It was so worth it.

As the season came to a close we all knew: The Cavs were headed to the playoffs for the first time in their history.

There have been a large number of Cleveland playoff teams in my life (mostly because I'm old, and not because of any raging success by the Browns). A few stand out. This team was one of them.

Listening to Joe Tait describe the team – they sounded like a bunch of unselfish guys.

The stats told the same story:

Jim Brewer: 10.7 shots per game, 11.5 PPG.
Jim Cleamons: 10.8 shots per game, 12.2 points.
Jim Chones: 15.3 shots, 15.8 points.
Bingo Smith: 13.8 shots, 13.6 points.
Dick Snyder: 10.7 shots, 12.6 points.
Campy Russell: 12.2 shots, 15.0 points.
Austin Carr: 9.6 shots, 10.1 points.

I haven't done any studies on shot distribution, but I'm willing to bet this was – statistically – one of the most unselfish teams ever.

A friend of mine recently told Jim Cleamons about my interest in that team. Cleamons said one thing that confirmed what I believed back then: "We didn't care who got the glory".

The Cavs finished one game ahead of the Washington Bullets. This gave them the home court advantage in the playoff series.

The Cavaliers first playoffs ever:

Game 1: The home court advantage was erased. Washington 100, Cleveland 95.

Game 2: Bingo Smith hit a 25 footer at the end. Cavs win, 80-79.

In Game 3 the Cavs actually won a game comfortably. 88-76.

Game 4, back at Washington, was a 109-98 Bullets win.

Game 5: The Bullets led 91-90 with 7 seconds to go. Elvin Hayes had two free throws. He missed both. Bingo Smith launched a shot that worked more like a pass to Jim Cleamons. Cleamons picked off the rebound under the basket and laid the ball in as time expired. Cavs 92, Bullets 91.

Game 6: The Cavs tried to seal the series on the road, but lost in overtime, 102-98.

Game 7: The game was tied at 85 with 24 seconds left. With 7 seconds left Dick Snyder drove to the lane and put up a beautiful 7 foot shot that banked off the backboard and through the net. The Bullets frantically tried to tie the game, but missed.

Cavs win the series, 4 games to 3. Two of the wins (games 2 and 5) were almost certain losses. This series was the perfect cap for the miracle of Richfield.

The Cavs, with all the momentum in the world, were set to face Boston in the conference finals. I no longer cared about Cowens, Havlicek or Silas. The Celtics were getting old, and the Cavs were on a roll.

Then it happened: Jim Chones broke his foot in a practice before the Boston series. Nate Thurmond and his 34-year-old knees were pressed in to full time duty.

Boston won the first two games, both in Boston Garden. The Cavs then won the first two at the Coliseum. I remember watching Game 5. It was a tight game. I kept thinking "Get this one, then we only need to win one in Boston..." But in the fourth quarter, Nate Thurmond fouled out. Boston went on to win the game, and game 6.

I was disappointed, but not terribly so. The entire season was a party.

Unfortunately, the hangover was about to set in...

THE HANGOVER (AKA THE TED STEPIEN YEARS)

There were two times in my life when I stopped rooting for a Cleveland professional sports team. Both were the fault of the owner.

Once was the Browns in 1996. Let's not go there.

The other time was 1982, courtesy of an owner who was even worse than Art Modell, if such a thing is possible, Theodore J. Stepien.

After the Miracle of Richfield, some of the players were lost:

In 1977 the Cavaliers lost Jim Cleamons as a free agent, but received Walt Frazier as compensation. Not bad.

In 1978 the Cavs lost Dick Snyder as a free agent, but received a third round draft pick as compensation. Bill Laimbeer was the choice. Again, not bad.

In 1979 Stan Albeck became the second head coach of the Cleveland Cavaliers. The Cavs were coming off a 30-52 record in the prior season.

Albeck immediately made changes: In September he sent the Cavs 1st round choice in 1980 to the San Diego Clippers for guard Randy Smith. Just before the start of the season Jim Chones was sent to Los Angeles for center Dave Robisch. A little while later Bingo Smith went to San Diego for a 3rd round draft choice.

The Cavs finished strong in 1980, winning 10 of their last 12 to finish at 37-45. They were third in offense, averaging 114 points per game. On January 29, 1980 they beat the Lakers 154-153 in 4 OT. I didn't get much sleep that night, preferring to listen to Joe Tait describe the action on WWWE.

At the end of the season I was optimistic. There was a young established star in 24-year-old Mike Mitchell who averaged 22 points per game. Randy Smith, one of the fastest guards I've ever seen, contributed 17.6 per game. Robisch was solid at center: 15 points and 8 rebounds per game.

Even better, Campy Russell was still there! Russell missed half of the season with injury, but averaged 18 per game when healthy. Add in young Kenny Carr (24 years old, 12 ppg), point guard Foots Walker, new center Bill Laimbeer and veteran Austin Carr, and things looked good heading in to 1980-81. They looked so good that owner Nick Mileti rewarded Albeck with a 3-year extension.

Then it happened: Ted Stepien bought the team.

In April 1980 Stepien bought controlling interest in the Cavs. Stepien's previous ownership experience was owner of the Cleveland Competitors Professional Softball team. That wasn't as useful as you might think. Even if you think it wasn't useful at all.

Almost immediately the red flags went up:

Red Flag #1: Shortly after buying the team Stepien noted that the reason the team wasn't drawing well was the fact that 10 of the 11 players on the roster were black. But these quotes were of course "taken out of context", and Stepien later noted that "I love my black players as much as my white ones". Right.

Red Flag #2: After taking over the team Stepien complained about the 3 year deal that Mileti gave Albeck, saying that he was unaware of this contract and if it had been up to him, Albeck would have gotten one year.

Albeck's deal had an out clause. In June 1980, he decided he couldn't stand Stepien, and exercised the out clause. Albeck took over at San Antonio.

Red Flag #3: As soon as Albeck left Stepien cried to the media, saying he was unaware of the out clause (well duh – if you were unaware of the contract…), and Albeck was leaving the team in the lurch.

Red Flag #4: Since Albeck was gone, Stepien promoted Bill Musselman to head coach. This was an absolute disaster. Muselman remains the worst head coach I've ever seen. And I saw Eric Mangini.

Red Flag #5: The Dallas Mavericks came into existence. In their expansion draft they took players who were considered the 9th best player by their current team. All NBA teams protected 8 players. Remember that: *The players that the Mavericks received were the 9th best on their respective teams.*

On May 28 the Mavericks drafted Austin Carr from the Cavaliers. This left Campy Russell and Foots Walker as my last real links to the miracle of Richfield. Still, we had Russell, Mitchell, Robisch, Laimbeer and Randy Smith. I was stupidly optimistic.

On June 20 Robisch was signed to a 4-year extension. He was a good center, and I was happy.

Red Flag#6 – the trades started:

On September 16 the Cavs traded their first round pick in 1984 to Dallas for Mike Bratz (the 9th best player on the 1979-80 Phoenix Suns). The Cavs were now without first round picks in 1982 and 1984.

On September 24, Foots Walker was sent to New Jersey for Roger Phegley.

On September 25, Campy Russell was sent packing in a 3-way trade that brought back forward Bill Robinzine. Robinzine played 8 games for the Cavaliers, logging a total of 83 minutes.

On October 30, Robinzine went to Dallas with first round draft picks in 1983 and 1986 for forward Richard Washington (9th best player on Milwaukee) and center Jerome Whitehead (9th best player on Utah).

One day later, the recently extended Dave Robisch was traded to Denver for Kim Hughes. Hughes averaged 7 minutes per game.

You might think that trading away Robisch would have left a vacancy for Whitehead at center. Nope. Whitehead played a total of 8 minutes before the Cavs cut him. The next season Whitehead averaged 18.8 points and 9.2 rebounds per game.

In December I put pencil to paper, and realized that, in three short months the Cavaliers had given up the following:

Dave Robisch
Campy Russell
First round picks in 1983, 1984 and 1986.

And in exchange they now had:

Richard Washington
Mike Bratz

The original 1981 and 1983 picks were gone, having been traded back in 1977 to Philadelphia for Terry Furlow. The Cavs did manage to get back a 1983 first round pick from Atlanta for Furlow in 1979, but that went to Dallas in the yard sale.

The 1982 first round pick was gone. The Cavs traded that pick to Los Angeles for a first round pick in 1980.

That meant that, as I sat there looking at the sorry roster of the Cavs at the end of 1980, their next first round pick was in the 1985 draft – my senior year in college.

On February 7, 1981, the Cavs took care of that nasty 1985 first round pick (and any hope I had of seeing them draft in the first round while I was in college) trading it and former number 1 (1980) Chad Kinch to Dallas for Geoff Huston. Huston lasted until December 7, 1984, when he was released.

The trade required the approval of the NBA, which had instituted a "Cleveland Trade Embargo". No trades without approval. But they approved this one. Apparently the NBA didn't want Dallas ripping off the Cavs without their official approval.

Red Flag #7:

By this point the Cavaliers had a dance squad, the Teddi Bears. Also, they had an official team polka.

Admittedly, I liked the Teddi Bears. Anything to keep my mind off the team.

Red Flag #8:

Stepien, a native of Pittsburgh (of course), announced that he was considering moving the team to Pittsburgh, or Cincinnati, or Louisville, or Minneapolis.

This was the start of a good thing; It motivated the eventual new owners of the Cavs, George and Gordon Gund, to take action to keep the team in Cleveland.

Okay, I give up:

In June 1981 I learned Joe Tait was gone. Tait, the legendary Cavaliers play by play man on WWWE, the man I listened to more than any other announcer growing up, the man who brought the 1976 Miracle of Richfield to life, was run out of town by Stepien.

If Tait couldn't take it, neither could I. I stopped watching. I stopped listening.

(Don't feel too bad for me – I went to college where the legal drinking age was 18. I found things to do with my time.)

But I digress. After I gave up, things just kept getting worse. I was still aware of the Cavaliers. I couldn't open the Plain Dealer and not read the Cavs news. The news was always bad.

In the summer of 1981 Stepien went on a spending spree, bringing in mediocre talent (center James Edwards, forward Scott Wedman and guards James Silas and Bobby Richardson) at a premium price.

In December 1981, the last good player in Cleveland, Mike Mitchell, was flipped to San Antonio for Ron Brewer and Reggie Johnson.

On January 20, 1982, addressing the fact that the Cavs record was 7-30, Stepien said: "It's (head coach Chuck) Daly's job to win with this talent. If he thinks it's not enough he's crazy."

Stepien, who was responsible for bringing in all the "talent" at the cost of all his first round picks through 1986, added "He (Daly) won't quit and I won't fire him." Daly was fired on March 8.

In July 1982, Stepien noted that the Cavs poor record (15-67) was due to players "habitual drug use". He didn't state which of the 23 players from the prior season were using.

Let's review:

- All of the good players and all of the draft picks were traded away for players that were not worthy of being protected in an expansion draft.
- The team had employed 23 players in the prior year.
- The team had a polka.
- The dance squad was named after the owner.

And we're supposed to believe **the players were the ones on drugs????**

In November, Stepien announced he would sell the Cavs. Don King said he was interested – but once that didn't pan out, I knew things would get better.

In December the Cavs traded Ron Brewer for World B. Free. Finally! A name I recognized!

In 1983, George and Gordon Gund bought the Cavaliers from Stepien. Almost immediately Joe Tait came back. So did I.

I've been a fan ever since.

Long after he's gone (he died in 2007), Stepien's legacy lives on, in the form of the "Ted Stepien Rule". The rule prohibits a team from trading first round picks in consecutive years.

1980s – A RECOVERY

In 1984 the Cavs drafted center Mel Turpin. Not a good pick.

In 1985 the Cavs drafted Charles Oakley. A good pick. They immediately traded him for power forward Keith Lee. Not a good trade.

The 1985 Cavs started the season 2-19. Coach George Karl decided to run the offense through World B. Free and things got a lot better in a hurry. Late in December they added Edgar Jones, a player who didn't do much in the box score, but was a fan favorite. The dude could dunk. Monstrously.

The Cavs finished 36-46 – good enough for 8th seed in the playoffs.

Some friends and I scored tickets to Game 3 of the Boston playoff series. In the section behind the basket.

The game was incredible. When the sound system blared the start of "We will rock you" (beat, beat, clap, beat, beat clap) we would yell "Ben Poquette" a tribute to the Cavs' forward from Central Michigan. When the sound system played "We are the World" it became a tribute to World B. Free.

(Yeah we knew it was written as a way to end world hunger, but come on – World B. Free was the man!)

The Cavs won, 105-98. The crowd was delirious.

To be fair, the Celtics were missing one player, Larry Bird. He was back at the hotel nursing a sore back.

Toward the end of the game, as 20,900 fans basked in the glory of beating the Celtics, 20,899 of them chanted "We want Bird! We want Bird!" I chanted "No we don't! No we don't!"

Come on, we won by 7 points! Larry Bird would have scored at least that many, right?

Sadly, the rest of the fans got what they wanted. Two days later Bird returned and scored 34, and the Cavs lost by 2 points. The Celtics won the series. The lesson is clear: Be careful what you wish for.

The 1985 Cavs were overachievers. They needed more talent.

They got that talent in 1986:

- With the number one overall choice they took center Brad Daugherty.
- They added guard Ron Harper with the 7th pick.
- Finally, just for good measure, they traded with Dallas to get the first pick in the second round. That pick was point guard Mark Price. Suck it Dallas, you owed us one.

Add to that 1985 second round pick Hot Rod Williams and the Cavs looked like they were set for success.

The team came together over the next couple of years.

In 1988 the new Cleveland Cavaliers stormed out the gate with a 40-point victory at Charlotte, and didn't really look back on their way to a 57-25 record, second best in the NBA. To put that in perspective – the NBA Champion Cavs of 2015-2016 won 57 games, and had the third best record.

18

Unfortunately for the Cavs the second best record in the NBA meant a third seed. In 1988, the top two seeds in each conference went to the division champions. The best record in the NBA belonged to the Detroit Pistons (63-19). The number two seed went to the New York Knicks (52-30).

The first round of the playoffs featured the #3 seed Cavs playing the Michael Jordan led Chicago Bulls in a best of 5 series. The Bulls were an up and coming team – but didn't scare me. After all, they had one really good player (Scottie Pippen was a rookie – I hadn't heard much about him). The Cavs had Ronnie Harper, Mark Price, Larry Nance, Brad Daugherty and Hot Rod Williams. The Cavs were 6-0 against the Bulls in the regular season. How much damage could Michael Jordan do?

Jordan AVERAGED 39.8 points per game in the series. 5 games, 199 points. He capped off the damage with a 44 point game 5, that included a game winning shot that – up until 2016 – was known as "The Shot" in Cleveland Sports lore.

In real time the shot itself was impressive. In slow motion it was amazing. Jordan jumps up to release his shot. Craig Ehlo flies past in an attempt to block. Jordan hangs in the air until Ehlo flies past, then lets go.

It was impressive. I was depressed.

My fiancée didn't understand how I could get so upset. We've been married for 26 years now, and she still doesn't understand. To be honest, neither do I. There is no logic to it. But from the moment the Cavs went out and drilled Charlotte in November I was emotionally invested.

I also tried telling myself that next year the Cavs would come back and knock off the Bulls and Pistons. On paper, it sounded reasonable. They had a great young team. The reality was:

1989-90: Brad Daugherty lost half the season to an injured foot, Ron Harper got traded for Danny Ferry, and they lost to the 76ers in the first round

1990-91: Mark Price sat close to a moving sign in Atlanta. It moved, he didn't, and he was lost for the season with a left knee injury. They missed the playoffs.

1991-92: Cavs won 57 games again, and make it to the conference finals. This time the 67-15 Bulls took them out in 6 games. On the upside – Jordan only averaged 31.7 this time.

1992-93: Cavs won 54 games. This time they drew the Bulls in the semi-finals. The Bulls had an off year, winning only 57 games. They hit their stride in the playoffs. Bulls 4-0.

1993-94: New coach Mike Fratello guided the Cavs to a 47-35 record, good enough to draw the Bulls in round one. Bulls sweep.

At this point I didn't think I could hate a Chicago team more than I hated the Bulls. In part that's because I figured the Cubs would never make the World Series.

Every team has a certain window of opportunity. This Cavs team window closed for good after 1994. Brad Daugherty retired at age 28 due to back problems. Larry Nance also retired. Mark Price and Hot Rod were traded away in 1995. Danny Ferry stayed around, playing with a variety of really good point guards (Terrell Brandon then Andre Miller).

In the late 1990s the Cavs spent several seasons in NBA purgatory – being just good enough to make the playoffs (and avoid a lottery pick) but nowhere near good enough to win a playoff series. They then went to a lower level of purgatory – bad enough to miss the playoffs, but still not so bad that they would get a load of ping pong balls in the lottery.

They had some name players in the 90s. Shawn Kemp made his way through Cleveland, fathered a few kids, ate a few Big Macs and moved on.

"Oh yeah – I remember that guy". Ten Cavs I forgot about before I wrote this book:

Luke Witte
Luol Deng
Ben Wallace
J. J. Hickson
Jamario Moon
Ira Newble

20

DeSagana Diop
Lee (Instant) Nailon
Andrew Bynum
Mike Miller

In 2002-2003 the Cavs got it right. They unloaded all talent, wound up 17-65, and got the ping pong ball that would lead to the greatest player in Cavs (if not NBA) history.

We could talk about the effect of LeBron leading the Cavs, then leaving the Cavs, and how we all felt, but suffice it to say:

1. I loved him when he was here.
2. I was pissed off when he left.
3. I was happy but still cautious when he came back.
4. And now – all is forgiven, and forgotten.

The only problem is – I wish I hadn't given away my LeBron jersey when he took his sabbatical in Miami.

AND THEN IT ENDED....

Officially the Cavs won the world championship on June 19, 2016.

In reality, it happened in January 2016.

On January 18 the Cavs lost to Golden State by a score of 132-98.

On January 22 the Cavs fired coach David Blatt. Ty Lue took over.

Very few fans (if any) believe that the Cavs would have won the NBA championship under Blatt.

The message was clear – we have a team that can win it all. Anything less is a disappointment.

I was shocked when the move was announced. But I was okay with it. If there was one thing the Cavs under Blatt proved it was that they couldn't beat the Warriors.

Things didn't come together right away. The Cavs were 30-11 under Blatt and 27-14 under Lue.

But 2016 wasn't about the regular season. The #1 seed in the East was almost a given. Besides – there was no guarantee that the Warriors would win the West. I was kind of hoping for an upset by San Antonio or (even better) Oklahoma City. An NBA title, however it came, would be just fine with me.

For a while it looked like I might get my wish. Steph Curry got hurt early on in the playoffs. He would be out for a couple of weeks. I never want to see someone get hurt. But given that he was hurt... Well, maybe Golden State would have to see how the playoffs worked when your point guard is out... The Cavs did in 2015.

I immediately started rooting for Portland. Were they within Steph Curry of being as good as the Warriors?

Not even close. Golden State won two at home. Portland won one at home.

Then Curry came back. 40 points on the road, and the Warriors won in overtime, 132-125.

The 2016 Steph Curry seemed like a different Curry. I always had a problem rooting against Golden State, because Curry seemed like a good guy, just doing his job. He was 6'3" – just an everyday guy who did his job very very well. His dad played for the Cavaliers. He was from Akron. What's not to like?

But in the 2016 playoffs, he was on the floor at Portland, hitting a 3 and taunting the Blazers fans "I'm back."

He was, in other words, going through a metamorphosis and becoming another Golden State ass.

Make room Draymond, we got another one.

And then there was the whole Mrs. Curry issue. Everything that went wrong was a conspiracy against her precious husband. And it all went on Twitter.

She started tweeting and I started thinking two words "Cici Boozer".

A part of me put an asterisk next to the 2015 finals. Yes, Golden State picked apart the Cavs in 6, but the Cavs were without Kyrie Irving (thanks to a game one season ending knee injury) and Kevin Love (thanks to the Boston thugs, specifically Kelly Olynyk, who pulled Love's arm out of his shoulder...). That part of me felt like a series against the Warriors with Irving and Love at full strength would be a great one.

But there was another part of me that wanted to see the 73-9 Warriors eliminated before the finals. The sooner and better. There were a lot of tough teams in the West (San Antonio for one), but the Warriors, a team that played in the tough west and won 73 games, was the toughest. If another team did the dirty work for the Cavs, well that was fine with me.

When Oklahoma City knocked off San Antonio I became a big Thunder fan. If the Thunder somehow managed to beat the Warriors, not only would the Cavs have an easier opponent, but they would also have home court advantage – based on the better regular season record.

I didn't hold out much hope. I read that someone calculated the Thunder had a 30% chance of winning the series. I thought "sounds a tad optimistic, but I'll take it."

The Thunder went in to Golden State and won game 1. I watched precisely one half of the game. Golden State led 60-47 at the half and I said "30% my ass" and went to bed. Too bad, because the Thunder owned the second half, and won 108-102.

Golden State took game 2. Steven Adams took a Draymond Green knee to the groin, in a nice preview of what was going to happen to Adams in game 3.

Which brings us right to game 3. In the midst of fighting for a rebound, Green did a kick that would make a Rockette envious. And he landed a foot right in the groin of Steven Adams. He was assessed a flagrant foul – which Steve Kerr didn't like. In fact, Kerr wanted the NBA to rescind the flagrant foul since limbs flail around (or in this case straight up and down) when trying to establish position. My guess is Kerr was pleading Green's case publicly, hoping to avoid a suspension.

From my point of view, this was an easy one. Not only was Green going to keep the flagrant foul, he was going to get suspended for one game.

Meanwhile... Over in Toronto... At the end of game 3 against the Raptors, Dhantay Jones hit Bismack Biyombo in the same spot. Same case could be made, Jones' arm was swinging behind him, and made contact.

Jones was suspended for one game.

Green was not suspended.

Line up 100 men and ask them – if you were forced to take one of those two shots, which one would you take? All 100 will take the hand from Jones over the foot from Green. Steve Kerr would take Jones over Green.

Green basically got off with only a flagrant foul. It was a flagrant 2 – which put him within one flagrant foul of a one game suspension. That would come to bite him later in the playoffs.

And bite him hard.

At just the right time.

Meanwhile, all the Thunder needed to do was hold the home court. I mean surely Kevin Durant could to that, right?

Then the Thunder got my hopes up. They went back to Oklahoma and beat the snot out of the Warriors twice in a row, 133-105 and 118-94. Just. One. More. Win.

It was not to be. Golden State took 3 in a row. Once again everyone was singing the Warriors' praises. Kevin Durant choked. One hopes that wasn't his last playoff choke.

The Cavs appeared to have peaked a little early. They blew out Detroit in 4, then swept Atlanta in 4. They put on what can best be described as Harlem Globetrotters vs. Washington Generals for the first two games of the Toronto series.

Then, in Toronto, the tables turned. The Raptors won twice.

Eventually the Cavs won the series 4 games to 2, but as the finals started I had a feeling that it would have been better to catch the Warriors a couple of weeks earlier

THE 2016 NBA FINALS:

Game one wasn't even close. Warriors 104, Cavs 89.

Game two made game one look close. Warriors 110, Cavs 77.

Which brings us to game 3. I thought "Wow. 4 and out." The Cavs looked mismatched. They were trying to run with the Warriors, and they were failing. Miserably.

What I didn't know was that Ty Lue had things figured out. He knew the Cavs couldn't slow down the Warriors and win. They proved that in 2015. The first two games just showed how fast the Cavs would need to be.

In Game 3 the Cavs were faster. Game 3 is one of those games I could watch over and over. It was as if Golden State missed the flight to Cleveland and the Atlanta Hawks filled in. Cleveland won 120-90.

I had just a candle of hope. If we could pull off the same thing in game 4 then all we needed was one win in Golden State…

The hope of a game 4 win lasted a little over one half. The Cavs led 55-50 at the half. Golden State dominated the second half and won 108-97.

One good thing happened in Game 4. In the midst of fighting for a rebound, LeBron stepped over Draymond Green, who had fallen on the floor. This put LeBron's nether regions within arm's length of Draymond. It was as if they said "Hit us Draymond… heard you wouldn't…"

Of course Aesha Curry thought that LeBron was baiting him. (She tweeted as much.)

If LeBron was baiting Draymond – it worked. One good ball tag later and Green had his 4th flagrant foul in the playoffs, and a ticket to any place other than Oracle Arena for Game 5.

In game 5 the Cavs had a new attitude. Nothing, and we mean NOTHING will be given to Golden State. Everything will be contested. Even a practice layup after the play is whistled dead. Steph Curry threw up a practice layup – and it was… REJECTED… By King James.

Aesha thought this was a bush league move. (She tweeted as much).

As earlier noted, Game 3 was my favorite Cavs game ever. That lasted right up until Game 6.

Let us now look back fondly at the first quarter of game 6.

J.R. Smith misses a 3 pointer.
Klay Thompson layup blocked by Kyrie Irving.
LeBron makes 1 of 2 free throws (1-0).
Harrison Barnes misses a 3 pointer.
Tristan Thompson makes 1 of 2 free throws (2-0).
Barnes misses a layup, gets the rebound. Klay Thompson misses a 3 pointer.
Kyrie jump shot (4-0).

Kyrie misses a 3 pointer.

Barnes misses a 3 pointer, LeBron steals the ball from Thompson and dunks (6-0)

After a timeout and a couple of missed shots, LeBron banks one home (8-0).

Green layup (8-2).

Kyrie 3 pointer (11-2).

Another Barnes miss and another LeBron dunk (13-2)

Curry a 3 pointer, then Klay Thompson makes a shot (13-7 and it looks okay for the Warriors).

Smith 3 pointer (16-7).

Warrior miss and Jefferson for 2 (18-7). Double digit lead.

Warrior miss and Kyrie for 2 (20-7).

Ezeli a layup (20-9).

And then for the last 3:30 things really got fun.

Tristan Thompson 2 free throws (22-9).

Klay Thompson misses a 3, Tristan Thompson a dunk (24-9).

Klay Thompson turns the ball over, LeBron a layup (26-9).

Livingston misses and Mo Williams adds a jump shot (28-9).

Ezeli turnover and Jefferson makes a free throw (29-9). 20 point lead.

Ezeli misses a rebound dunk, Tristan Thompson another dunk (31-9).

Two more points for Golden State and the quarter is over. Cavs lead 31-11.

The sideline reporter interviews coach Kerr, who basically does his best Kevin Bacon / Animal House "Remain calm, all is well."

Any time you win a quarter 31-11 you are in good shape. I don't care what Kerr says.

LeBron James Game 6 numbers: 41 points. Over the last two games he's now averaging 41 points a game. Not. Too. Shabby. 9 in the first quarter when the game was essentially won.

The reigning MVP Game 6 Numbers: 30 points. 2 in the first quarter when the game was essentially lost.

Fun play of the game:

Well, there were so many, but my personal favorite has to be the J.R. Smith behind the back no look alley oop to LeBron for the slam. The Cavs were leading 74-57. On yet another fast break Kyrie throws the ball to J.R. who dribbles, then flips the ball up behind his head to LeBron. It was a thing of beauty from every angle. I've seen that play 100 times. Not nearly enough.

And now: The Game 7 to end all Game 7s.

Up to this point there had only been one other time in my life where a Cleveland victory would mean a championship (the 1997 World Series).

First quarter: There is a lot of back and forth. Golden State misses a couple of wipe open 3s early. That always helps. The Cavs don't hit on a single 3 point shot in the first.

At one point Steph Curry (RMVP) brings the ball up with the Warriors leading 13-10. Richard Jefferson picks his pocket, then scores two on the other end.

(This one play was probably the reason that all of Cavs nation said "NOOOOOO!" when Jefferson said he was going to retire after the season. Thankfully, he listened.)

At the end of the first quarter the Warriors bring in Anderson Varajao. This helps the Cavs' offense. New game plan: Just give it to the guy Andy's trying to cover.

Varajao was always one of my favorite Cavaliers. I love his sideshow Bob hair. Always have. But at this point in his career, he helps the opponents when he's out there.

Late in the first quarter he tries to draw a charge. I'm not sure if anyone keeps stats for most charges drawn with good acting, but I'll bet Andy's right up there in the all-time list. This time it doesn't work. The call is blocking and Kevin Love hits two free throws.

End of First Quarter: Cavaliers 23, Warriors 22.

The Cavs were 0 for 4 from 3-point range. The Warriors were 5 for 10. This is as big of a lead as anyone could reasonably hope for.

The 2nd quarter:

When he isn't kicking people in the balls, Draymond Green is a pretty good basketball player. 32 points, 15 rebounds and 9 assists for the game – and it felt like most of them happened in the second quarter.

Fun play of the quarter: Early on the Warriors (leading 26-25) are on a fast break. Draymond tries to pass to the right, but LeBron picks it off, and calmly throws the ball the length of the floor to Mo Williams for a layup. Two seconds – one steal, one assist. That's how you wind up leading the series in all five major categories.

The Cavs keep throwing up 3s. They keep missing. I keep saying "Eventually they'll fall." Fortunately, I'm right. At 7:03 in the quarter Iman Shumpert hits a 3 from the corner. As an added bonus Shaun Livingston slaps him in the hand after he lets go of the ball. Four-point play.

Things go downhill after that. Draymond Green scores 9 points in a row. Then Barbosa hits a 3. (Isn't he the bad guy in Pirates of the Caribbean?). This concerns me. When the Warriors are getting 3s from these guys it becomes a waiting game for Curry and Thompson to get started.

At the half it's Golden State 49, Cleveland 42. I'm not happy, but I do take consolation in one fact: Golden State has ten 3s so far. Cleveland has just one. That's a 27 point difference right there. If we can just get our 3s to start dropping – we still have a chance.

The 3rd quarter:

Early on in the third quarter the Warriors extend the lead to 8 points. Klay Thompson is getting hot. I'm getting worried.

J.R. Smith says "Don't worry Phil."

10:08 – J.R. Smith for 3!
9:34 – J.R. Smith for another 3!
8:53 – Kyrie layup.

Just like that – we're tied. A quick 8-0 run. The exact kind of run I had to endure watching last year. Now we're the team with instant offense.

The third quarter continues with the back and forth spurts. Warriors score 5 in a row. Cavs answer with 11 in a row. With 3:18 the Cavs now lead 70-63. A little over one minute later it's tied at 71.

This game is wearing me out.

End of third quarter: Golden State 76, Cleveland 75.

A 4th Quarter to end all 4th Quarters:

With 5:37 left Draymond Green grabs an offensive rebound and puts it back in for a 4-point lead (87-83). Something needs to happen.

Something did – LeBron got a one on one matchup with Festus Ezeli. As Festus slaps LeBron the king throws up a 3 point shot.

LeBron, who hasn't made a 3 point shot yet, misses this one too. But he goes to the line and knocks down all 3 free throws. (87-86).

Steph Curry (the reigning NBA MVP) then executes a beautiful behind the back pass to someone in the front row. Turnover. Cavs ball.

This time LeBron does NOT miss the 3. Cavs lead, 89-87.

At 4:39 left Klay Thompson scores what will be the last points that the high scoring Warriors get for the night. 89-89.

For the next 3 minutes no one scores. Missed shots, turnovers, blocked shots, non-shooting fouls.

I am freaking out.

Then it happened.

Andre Iguodala takes off. He's headed in for a dunk. I'm thinking "What will we call this one? The almost?" J.R. Smith moves to contest but NOT foul. It slows Iguodala down just long enough for a new "The" event. The Chasedown. From out of nowhere, LeBron chases him down, and blocks the layup. Cleanly. So clean that even Steve Kerr couldn't complain and Aesha couldn't tweet.

It was a "WOW!" moment. But in that moment, I had no idea how impressive the Chasedown really was.

Two weeks later we were eating at Firehouse Subs. ESPN replayed the Chasedown. My son asked "Dad, how did LeBron DO that?" I said "I don't know..."

Almost on cue ESPN went into explaining the science. LeBron ran at over 20 miles per hour. J.R. slowed Iguodala up by 0.2 seconds – just enough for LeBron to make up the last 15 feet and block the ball.

As ESPN went to an ad my son asked "Yeah dad, but how did LeBron DO that?"

And even after seeing the science behind it – I don't understand how LeBron did it. I mean... If I took off with a 22 foot head start against LeBron I'm certain he would catch me by the other end of the court. But he made up 22 feet against an NBA player. Just by being in the NBA that guarantees the guy with the 22 foot lead is one of the top 0.1% of all athletes in the world. LeBron James chased down one of the top athletes in the world.

I said "I don't know how he did it son. But I'm glad he did."

After the Chasedown the game is still tied at 89. Another "The" was needed. Enter Kyrie Irving. With Steph Curry draped all over him Irving hits a 3 that will – Jordan be damned - forever be known as "The Shot".

It's now Curry's turn. Golden State executes a trap and gets the matchup they wanted – Kevin Love against Curry. Curry quickly moves left and sees Kevin Love standing right in front of him. Curry moves right and sees... Kevin Love right in front of him. In desperation Curry throws up... a 3 which missed badly. If I had to nickname it I would call it "The Scud".

Tristan Thompson rebounds. The Cavs have the ball and a 3-point lead with 34 seconds to go.

Each team still has one foul to give. The Cavs can run the game clock down to 10 seconds. The Warriors, in keeping with their mantra of "screw it up" foul with 18 seconds remaining – and only 8 on the shot clock. The shot clock was reset to 14 seconds. In effect the Warriors said "Here Cavs… Have another 6 seconds."

As it turned out, the Cavs don't use their entire 14 seconds. With 10 seconds to go LeBron breaks free and goes to the rim with what will be a championship slam. Draymond Green wisely (geez I can't believe I actually said those 3 words in succession) fouls LeBron. James lands hard and doesn't get right up.

At this point I'm thinking "Oh no. Will this be 'THE FOUL?' Or 'THE ANKLE'? I'm holding my breath. If LeBron can get up off the floor and make one free throw, the game is effectively over.

He missed the first free throw. I don't think I've drawn a breath for 2 minutes at this point.

Second free throw. To quote the great Joe Tait "sights it, shoots it, got it!"

Warriors ball with 10 seconds left.

And the Cavs, unlike the Warriors, effectively use their free foul. They use it as soon as the Warriors move the ball inside the 3-point line. (No one was going to foul and risk a 4 point play). The Warriors are now forced to inbound again with 7 seconds left.

Two desperation 3 point misses later, and the clock reads :00.

And with that the Cavs completed The Comeback. Two wins in OraCLE arena. It was the "THE" to end all "THEs".

The post-game show was awesome. J.R. Smith gave one of the greatest press conferences ever. Then he took his shirt off. As far as I know, he hasn't worn a shirt since. I'm fine with that. Win a championship – shirts are optional.

The Cavs magic immediately rubbed off on the Indians

For the Indians, it lasted 14 games – a club record winning streak. It lasted into the playoffs and all the way to Game 7 in the World Series. It was a great run, one like never before.

PART TWO: THE INDIANS

"The Tribe – this is my team!" – Written on a scarf in my closet, and words I actually heard Joe Walsh yell at a concert in Cleveland Municipal stadium

June 2016 was a magical time in Cleveland. The Cavs, as mentioned, turned a deficit into a championship.

The Indians beat the White Sox in a walk-off, 3-2.
And then the beat the White Sox again.
And again.

And they just kept winning. A club record 14 game winning streak. Game 14 was one of the season's best: Indians 2, Blue Jays 1 in 19 innings. The win went to Trevor Bauer. The loss went to Blue Jays' second baseman turned pitcher Darwin Barney. The next day the bullpen lost a 1 run lead. The day after that the Indians lost to the Blue Jays 17-1, just to make sure everyone knew the winning streak was over. Then they got back to the business of winning the division.

As far as Toronto went: The Indians had the last laugh.

2016 was the kind of season I could only dream of back when I first became an Indians fan.

A FAN IS BORN – THE CEDAR POINT HELMET

It started in June 1970. I stood at the souvenir stand at Cedar Point in Sandusky Ohio. My parents told me I could buy a plastic batting helmet. The souvenir stand had two helmets: The Cleveland Indians helmet: Blue with a red "C" on it., and the Detroit Tigers helmet: Dark blue with a white script D on it.

Detroit won the 1968 World Series. Cleveland hadn't won a World Series since 1948. The Tigers were consistently at or near the top of the American League. Cleveland was consistently near the bottom. Detroit featured Hall of Famer Al Kaline, slugging first baseman Norm Cash (acquired in a trade with Cleveland), pitcher Mickey Lolich, catcher Bill Freehan and a host of role players that were heads and shoulders over their Cleveland counterparts.

I didn't know any of that.

Detroit games were broadcast on Channel 11 from Toledo. Cleveland games were on Channel 8 from Cleveland. Our antenna pulled in Toledo better than Cleveland.

I didn't know that either.

In fact, I didn't even know their nicknames. Tiger vs. Indian? I shudder to think what might have happened had I known.

My choice came down to this: Did I like the red C or the white D?

I liked the red C. I chose the Indians helmet.

In that moment, Cleveland – an hour east of my real hometown - became my adopted hometown.

From then on I lived and died with Cleveland's sports teams. My love for the Indians, Browns and Cavaliers outlasted the helmet.

A FAN'S LIFE – THE CEDAR POINT HELMET BITES THE DUST.

The Indians won but August 28, 1971 was still a bad day for me.

The Indians and Twins were on TV. I put on my Cedar Point plastic "Batting helmet", which was more like an ill-fitting uncomfortable plastic head decoration than a real batting helmet (there was a huge warning to that effect on the inside of the helmet), and sat down to watch the Indians take on the Minnesota Twins.

The Twins got off to a quick 3-0 lead. In the second, John Lowenstein, hitting a robust .187 at the time, hit a home run to cut the lead to 3-2. The Twins responded with 3 in the top of the third, turning it to a 6-2 lead. Ray Fosse, one of my earliest heroes (and fully recovered from the Pete Rose all-star incident) hit a grand slam to tie things up in the bottom of the third.

The Twins tacked on 2 more in the 4th, taking an 8-6 lead.

One inning later, with the score 8-6, Graig Nettles – my favorite player - stepped up. He sent a drive to the deepest part of the ballpark. The center fielder for the Twins - one Jim Nettles - went back to the fence and robbed his brother of a home run. Man, was I disappointed! Apparently, I wasn't the only one. Graig Nettles was pissed. He threw his helmet across the field.

Apparently back in 1971 there was some unwritten rule that: If you are a struggling center fielder you should stand there and watch the ball go out if it was your brother that hit it.

Fast forward to the 6th inning. Vada Pinson hits a 3 run home run. Indians take a 9-8 lead, which they hold. Tribe wins! Tribe wins!

As was my custom I went out to the yard and re-enacted my favorite part of the game. Which part did I pick? Pinson's game winner? Nope. My hero Ray Fosse's grand salami? Afraid not. The sub-Mendoza Lowenstein's home run? Never.

The favorite part that I re-enacted was Graig Nettles hitting a fly ball to the deepest part of the park, and watching my brother (my imaginary brother – my real brother wasn't available for the re-enactment) catch the ball. Then, just to make sure I got the re-enactment correct, I threw my batting helmet across the yard.

Remember when I said that the helmet wasn't a "batting" helmet? That's because if it were hit with a baseball it would shatter. I never hit one with a baseball, but I still feel fairly certain that's what would happen. Baseballs are harder than the grass in our yard. And when the helmet hit the grass, thrown with all the might an 8-year-old could muster, it cracked.

When comedians made jokes about my adopted hometown of Cleveland, I didn't laugh. And there were plenty of things to make jokes about. In 1972, mayor Ralph Perk tried to use a blowtorch. His hair caught on fire. Multiple times in the 1950s and 1960s the Cuyahoga River caught on fire.

The mayor's hair was on fire. The river was on fire. The only things that weren't on fire in Cleveland were the sports teams.

The Tribe was, is and always has been my team. I really like the Cavs. I like the Browns (Well I try to). But I love the Indians. Growing up I had a tennis ball and a glove. We had a barn. Every time the weather was good enough, I was throwing the ball off the barn and catching it. I was Gaylord Perry. I was Dennis Eckersley. I was Wayne Garland. (I got traded a lot, so I had to assume new roles). When winter came I went inside and threw the ball against the garage door. The tennis ball marks stayed there until mom and dad replaced the doors 20 years later.

The Indians were not a pretty sight in the 1970s. One of the reasons was their standing, at or near the bottom of the AL East. Another was the uniforms. One of the Tribe uniforms featured red shirts with red pants. Boog Powell stood on first base looking like a blood clot.

I liked Boog. He was a larger than life figure who could hit the ball a country mile. When the Indians traded Dave Duncan for Boog in 1975 I was thrilled. A former MVP – someone I had seen playing in the World Series – and he was ours!

Boog represented something that the Indians were missing since the dreaded Graig Nettles trade of 1973. On a team filled with John Lowensteins and Frank Duffys (Wait a minute... How do you spell the plural of "Duffy"? Duffies?) Boog represented someone famous. Someone I had watched in October.

Most of my year was spent listening to the games on AM radio. If I listened to a game on the Fremont station, I could only listen until sundown. At that point the local AM stations went off the air. Bigger AM stations (like WWWE, 1100 Cleveland) stayed on past sundown. Once I found WWWE my games were no longer called due to darkness.
The occasional treat was actually watching the Indians on TV - channel 8 (later 43). Channel 8's main camera was positioned above and behind home plate. I grew up watching pitches come from the pitcher to the batter

– top to bottom of the screen. Watching a game on TV from behind the pitcher was reserved for special occasions like the All Star game, the World Series, or occasionally the Saturday Game of the week... the "special games"

Players who were in the "special games" were automatically elevated in my opinion. If the Indians got enough of those players – they would play in the series. That was my theory anyway.

Boog Powell came with the required "special game" pedigree. Player manager Frank Robinson was another. I figured adding them to a team with Gaylord Perry meant we were destined to win the division.

That's exactly what happened. For one day anyway. On opening day Robinson hit a home run in the first. Boog went 3 for 3 with a double and a home run. Perry threw a complete game. Indians 5 Yankees 3.

Boog was one player that didn't disappoint me. In 1975 he launched 27 home runs. It wasn't enough of course. The Indians finished 79-80, fourth place.

Even when he was running around the bases after a home run – Boog Powell in a blood red uniform was not a pretty sight. Come to think of it, George Clooney would have looked ugly in that uniform. They were awful.

For most of my life the Indians performance matched the ugliness of the red uniforms. Occasionally they would flirt with success and finish around .500. In 1986 they went 84-78. In one of the more famous instances of the "Sports Illustrated curse" the Tribe graced the cover of the 1987 Baseball Preview issue. Outfielders Cory Snyder and Joe Carter were on the cover with the title "Indian Uprising." I was excited. They had good hitting. They had two knuckleballers (Tom Candiotti and Phil Niekro). They had 21 year old Greg Swindell. And they added Steve Carlton just before the season started.

The 1987 Indians finished 61-101.

"Oh yeah, I remember that guy". **Ten Indians I forgot about before I wrote this book:**

Steve Carlton (Indian for a little while)
Pat Tabler (Mr. bases loaded)
Doug Jones (the closer with a 68 mph change up)
George Vukovich (owned Dan Petry)
Jamie Quick (1 at bat, 1 home run – Indians career slugging percentage of 4.000)
Brook Jacoby (came from Atlanta with Brett Butler)
Keith Hernandez (after his Seinfeld appearance)
Ellis Burks
Jeromy Burnitz (traded him for Kevin Seitzer)
Kosuke Fukudome (Atlanta got the Georgia dome, we got the Fukudome).

From 1970 to the early 1990s the roster was a revolving door. Sam McDowell leaves and Gaylord Perry joins. Perry leaves and Jim Bibby, Jackie Brown and Rick Waits join. Jackie Brown goes to Montreal for Andre Thornton. Waits and Rick Manning go to Milwaukee for Gorman Thomas. Thomas to Seattle for Tony Bernazard.

It felt like that was the way a team operated. I never stopped to think about teams like the Dodgers – who had the same starting infield for 8 years (Cey, Russell, Lopes and Garvey) or Cincinnati, where Sparky Anderson put Rose / Morgan / Griffey / Bench / Perez on his lineup card every day.

Constant trades plus a dash of incompetence equaled the Indians of my youth.

Dash of incompetence? Who am I kidding? It was a truckload.

In 1978 the Indians signed 22-year-old Rick Manning to a 5 year $1.5 million contract. This on the heels of a season where he injured his back and hit .226, recorded a .282 on base percentage and a slugging percentage of .337. He managed 68 games for the year.

Still, the Indians were FORCED to sign him to a large contract, because of a clerical error.

The Indians sent contract proposals to Manning and pitchers Don Hood and Tom Buskey that called for 25% pay cuts. The labor agreement at the time said that the maximum pay cut was 20%. All three players sued to become free agents.

Indians GM Gabe Paul called it a clerical error. Clerical error? How exactly do you multiply by 0.75 instead of 0.8 three separate times?

At any rate, Paul put up way more money than he had intended to keep Manning around. Manning was young, an outstanding defensive centerfielder, and, up until the back injury, a very good hitter. But they could have paid him $44,000 (20 percent pay cut) in 1978. Instead they gave him $259,000.

That was dumb. This was dumber:

On March 6, 1978, pitcher Jim Bibby was declared a free agent. His 1977 contract with the Indians included a $10,000 bonus if he made at least 30 starts. He made exactly 30 starts. The Indians failed to pay Bibby the money, and while the team was in spring training for the 1978 season, an arbitrator made Bibby a free agent.

What was the Indians' defense? We thought 30 was less than 30? We meant to send him a check? We were out of money after we screwed up the Rick Manning contract?

The Indians were hopeful they could re-sign Bibby. (Yeah, we tried to cheat him out of 10 large, but we believe he'll come back). In a related story, I'm hopeful that the people from Publishers Clearing House knock on my door with ten million dollars.

Bibby took a little time off then signed with Pittsburgh on May 15. He went 39-17 for the Pirates over the next 3 years and earned a World Series ring.

And the knock on my door was a missionary.

But I digress.

None of this mattered to me. The Indians were my team. When outfielder Jim Norris and first base coach Joe Nossek made an appearance at

Holzapfel's Sporting Goods in downtown Sandusky, I was there. I got there early to beat the line that never materialized. I got to talk to Jim Norris! And he pointed at Joe Nossek and said "Do you know who this is?" I said "Yeah, the greatest sign stealer in baseball history!"

I still have the autographed ball.

I also have autographs from Paul Dade ("I can't be a star man, my number is 00".), Walt Williams. The Williams one happened at a basketball game. On our high school basketball floor!

A FAN'S LIFE - THE BUDDY BELL STORY

The Indians - looking to garner some fan interest - annually fielded a team of basketball players that traveled from school to school and took on local "legends".

On January 8, 1974 they played at my high school.

The local "legends" were the best of my high school. Players from prior teams – teams that won a conference title. Some of them were all-conference, perhaps even honorable mention all-state of Ohio.

The Indians' basketball team was composed of major league players. The Indians team had role players. That said, they were role players in the major leagues. For example: The point guard was Walt "No Neck" Williams. He was only 5'6" – a 4th outfielder on a second division team. But like all of the players on the team, Walt was an outstanding athlete.

The one exception to the "no one you've ever heard of" rule: Buddy Bell. Bell was fresh off a rookie season where - at age 21 - he started 156 games at third base and hit 14 home runs. He was a central part of a young lineup, featuring up and coming hitters Oscar Gamble (age 23), George Hendrick (23), Charley Spikes (23) and Chris Chambliss (24).

Suffice it to say, the Indians won. Even though they were baseball players, they were all around athletes. Athletes who were likely all state in multiple sports. Everything went the Indians way until the second half, when Bell hurt his right knee. He sat out the rest of the game, ice pack on his knee.

Fast forward to spring training: On March 21 Bell's knee buckled during a game. The papers insisted it was "unrelated to a knee injury he suffered while playing basketball on January 8". Every time I opened the paper, it said "Bell's knee is bothering him, but it's unrelated to the knee injury he suffered while playing basketball on January 8." Well, then stop mentioning it!

On May 21 Bell hurt the knee again. The Indians, doing their best Kevin Bacon in Animal House, ("Remain calm, all is well") up till then, finally put Bell on the DL on June 2.

On August 10, he injured the knee again, and went on the 21-day disabled list. The article again mentioned his knee injury suffered playing basketball on January 8. I was starting to feel personally responsible. "Bell injured his knee, but it isn't related to the January 8 incident where he played basketball just to entertain that selfish sixth grader Phil Barth …"

Bell had knee surgery during the offseason. This was the first of 10 knee surgeries (through 2000). Mind you, some were on the left knee, so they aren't all my fault.

Even though playoffs seemed to be off limits, there were some really memorable moments. On May 15, 1981 Lenny Barker took the mound in Cleveland and threw a perfect game against the Toronto Blue Jays. It was on TV. I was playing euchre with a bunch of buddies. Beer was being consumed (18 was legal back then). At one point someone said "Are the Indians playing?" The answer "Yeah, but the batteries in my radio are dead." Televised Indians games were rare. We didn't even think about turning on the TV. We sat there playing until someone stopped by and said "Did you not watch the game?"

Oops.

I made up for it by watching the re-broadcast (midnight to 2am) later that summer.

As bad as that was, I made it worse later in the summer. In addition to selling fishing equipment, our family friend Bill Baumler ran fishing charters. He called my mom and said "I'm taking Lenny Barker fishing tomorrow. Do your boys want to go?"

My brother was in. I said "I just started a new job so I'll have to pass."

I was honest. I was industrious. I was a moron.

If ever there was a time to call in sick…

My brother rubbed it in for a while. My response: "Keep it up buddy... I'll go all Graig Nettles on you yet."

After two decades of wandering in the dessert the Indians turned things around in the early 1990s.

They built a foundation with some great draft picks (Albert Belle, Manny Ramirez, Jim Thome, Charlie Nagy and later C.C. Sabathia).

They also made some outstanding trades to add more talent: Catcher Eddie Taubensee to Houston for Kenny Lofton. Outfielder Joe Carter to San Diego for Carlos Baerga and Sandy Alomar, Jr.

In 1994 the Indians moved in to their new home – Jacobs Field. They added some veterans to make sure it was a grand opening:

Shortstop Omar Vizquel came from Seattle for .Felix Fermin and Reggie Jefferson.
Pitcher Dennis Martinez and DH Eddie Murray signed as free agents.

The tribe featured a lineup with firepower from top to bottom. After 111 games the only hitter who wasn't in double figures for home runs was Omar Vizquel. Albert Belle led the team with 36. Rookie Jim Thome had 20 more. Manny Ramirez had a slugging percentage of .521 – FIFTH best on the team. (Thome was .523, Baerga was .525, Lofton was .536 and Belle was .721).

Wait a minute… Kenny Lofton? The leadoff hitter? Yep – 32 doubles, 9 triples, 12 home runs and a .349 batting average – to go with 60 stolen bases. All in 111 games.

There was one small problem. After 111 games the 1994 season ended. A strike wiped out the rest of the year, including the playoffs and World Series. The Indians finished in second place in the AL Central, one game behind the White Sox, and would have qualified for the wild card.

1995 – AFTER A 41 YEAR BREAK THE TRIBE IS IN THE PLAYOFFS!

After the strike was resolved in early 1995 the Indians made a move that convinced me they were going to win the World Series. On April 8 the Indians signed my favorite pitcher – fellow Bowling Green Falcon Orel Hershiser.

I knew big things were ahead. But in my most optimistic view I couldn't see what was coming:

- A record of 100-44.
- Albert Belle hitting 50 home runs and 50 doubles.
- A starting lineup where only Omar Vizquel had an OPS under .800
- Jose Mesa saving 46 games.
- A division clinched on September 8.
- A team that finished 30 games ahead of the second place Royals.
- 12 walk off wins.
- 13-0 in extra innings.

No game was ever over for this team.

On June 4 the Indians trailed Toronto 8-0. Final score: Indians 9, Blue Jays 8. Paul Sorrento with a 2 out 2 run home run in the bottom of the ninth.

On July 16 the Indians were behind 4-3 with 2 outs in the 9th. In what became known as the "Wow!" game Dennis Eckersley gave up a 2 run blast to Manny Ramirez. The cameras caught Eckersley saying "WOW" as he walked off the field.

Two days later Albert Belle launched a game winning grand slam off Lee Smith.

No reliever was safe. Even future hall of famers.

1995 was a great year for me. But the Tribe could have gone 0-162 and it still would have been a great year. On July 4, 1995 we had our first son - Kenny. He was designated my "baseball buddy". We immediately dressed him in Tribe clothing.

In October my baseball buddy and I got ready for something neither of us had experienced: The Cleveland Indians in the playoffs!

Victim number one - the Boston Red Sox

It's hard to imagine now, but the Divisional playoffs in 1995 only had regional coverage. The Cincinnati Reds were also in the playoffs (that's hard to imagine now too). Living in the Cincinnati area, that meant I got the Reds / Dodgers series. That meant the first Indians playoff game in my lifetime would be radio only for me.

I was listening during the 11th inning when Tim Naehring hit a home run to put Boston up 5-4.

I was listening during the bottom of the 11th when Albert Belle answered with a home run. Boston manager Kevin Kennedy accused Belle of corking the bat. Sadly, I could only listen to the announcers describe Belle looking at Kennedy and pointing at his huge bicep.

Why would anyone accuse Albert Belle of corking the bat?

In a July 15, 1994 game against the White Sox, Albert Belle's bat was confiscated and placed in the locked umpire dressing room. Indians pitcher Jason Grimsley crawled through the stadium ceiling in to the umpire's dressing room with a replacement bat. It was like an episode of Hogan's Heroes.

The idea didn't work, for a couple of reasons:

1. They didn't replace like for like. They replaced an Albert Belle model with a Paul Sorrento model. The reason for this? Albert Belle had corked every one of his bats. Every. Last. One. He didn't even save one just in case.

This is like replacing Kinchloe in the cooler with Louie LeBeau… it might work on TV, but…

2. The umpires were smarter than Sgt. Schultz and Col. Klink. They said "Hmmm. Paul Sorrento… isn't he the Italian guy that plays first base for them? I don't think that's who we busted…"

Belle got a 10-day suspension, later reduced to 7 days.

I listened all the way to the 13th inning. That's when Tony Pena – he of the 5 home runs all season – got a green light on a 3-0 pitch and hit a home run to end the game.

One of the things I loved about the 1990s Indians under Mike Hargrove was their total freedom to swing away on 3-0. In 1996 I watched as Nigel

Wilson – 0 for his first 25 career at bats – hit a 3-0 pitch out for a home run. The message was clear – if Nigel Wilson can swing 3-0 – anyone can. No pitcher got a freebie on 3-0 when Hargrove ran the show.

I'll also admit – I'm a Mike Hargrove fan boy. When he played for the Indians, Hargrove was my favorite player. He was called "The Human rain delay". He would step out of the box after every pitch and go through a routine of adjusting his batting gloves, his belt, his shoulder, touching his helmet, etc. Even some Indians fans hated it. But he worked pitchers to death, and usually was near the league lead in walks and on base percentage.

The same attention to details and looking for every advantage that made Hargrove such an annoying hitter (to some) made him the perfect manager for the Indians.

Game one final score: Indians 5, Red Sox 4

In game two Orel Hershiser went 7 innings and the Indians shut out the Sox. Eddie Murray had a home run. The Red Sox managed 3 hits.

Game two final score: Indians 4, Red Sox 0.

Game 3 was a blowout – Indians 8, Red Sox 2. Tim Wakefield started for the Red Sox. Jim Thome went yard for the Tribe.

The Boston series ended after 3 games. So did the regional coverage. From there on it was all televised playoff games.

Victim number two – The Seattle Mariners:

Seattle was managed by Lou Pinella – a former Reds manager, former Kansas City Royal, and... If you went back far enough in history – a former Cleveland Indian.

Pinella had one big thing in his favor – specifically a 6'10" tall big thing: Randy Johnson.

Fortunately for the Indians Johnson had to come in for 3 innings in game five of the Mariners/Yankees divisional playoffs. This was fortunate for two reasons:

1. It meant Johnson wouldn't start game one of the ALCS, and
2. It meant the Yankees lost.

My baseball buddy was there by my side. Specifically, he was there on my chest. Kenny was sometimes a colicky baby. We had nights where we took turns walking him. But baseball was the ultimate calm down for him. He would lay up against my chest. Every game in the Seattle series was a tight one. I could feel my heart beating at times. So could Kenny. The rhythm would put him to sleep for the entire game. Beth would be asleep on the couch, Kenny would be asleep on my chest, and I would be in the chair, glued to the TV.

The Mariners won game one in Seattle, 3-2. This wasn't good because we threw our ace (Dennis Martinez) and Seattle threw Bob Wolcott.

The Tribe came back and won game 2, 5-2. Orel Hershiser!

Seattle won game 3 in Cleveland. I expected this, because Randy Johnson was on the mound. What I didn't expect was the game going to extra innings, and Jay Buhner hitting a home run to win it 5-2.

In game 4, rent-a-pitcher Ken Hill took the mound for the Indians and threw a 7-0 shutout. Murray hit a home run in the first, Thome hit one in the third. No stress, no mess. Series tied at 2.

Game 5 was a good one for my baseball buddy. Indians were down 2-1 in the sixth when Thome hit a 2 run home run. Indians held on for a 3-2 win.

Game 6 was Randy Johnson vs. Dennis Martinez. Indians won with an error assisted run in the fifth, a passed ball assisted run in the 8th, and a Carlos Baerga home run. Indians 4, Mariners 0.

Bring on the Braves!

As game one started we were spending the weekend at a cabin in Oglebay Park in Wheeling West Virginia. We were celebrating my parents' anniversary a little late, and our wedding anniversary a little early.

Before the series started I kept hearing the warning from the media: Good pitching beats good hitting. The Braves had a rotation for the ages: Greg Maddux, Tom Glavine, John Smoltz and Steve Avery.

Still, I was optimistic. For every great Braves pitcher, the Indians had an equally incredible hitter. Besides – Dennis Eckersley hadn't stopped the Tribe. Ditto for Lee Smith.

Game one – the first Cleveland World Series game in 31 years!

In the first inning of game one the Indians proved my point. Kenny Lofton reached on an error, stole second, stole third and scored on a ground out. The Indians scored without a hit! I knew great things were ahead.

I went to the refrigerator, grabbed a beer and announced: "I'm having a beer for every run the Indians score tonight! It's a good thing we bought a case."

Sadly, a 6 pack would have been more than enough. For the entire weekend.

For the next 8 innings Greg Maddux showed that good pitching can indeed beat good hitting.

After about 5 innings I went back to the refrigerator. I was tired of waiting on the Indians for my second beer.

Final score: Braves 3, Indians 2. The Indians managed 2 hits all night. Maddux was dominant: a complete game victory.

Game 2 – If you liked Maddux, you'll love Glavine.

The Indians again jumped out to a lead (this time 2-0) but again lost, 4-3. The low point for Indians fans happened in the 8th inning. The Tribe was down 4-3 when Manny Ramirez drew a walk. Jim Thome was at the plate. I had seen this so many times – Thome a home run to win it. Apparently Manny expected that too. He certainly didn't expect catcher Javy Lopez to throw down to first base. Picked off. Inning over.

This entire game just felt like a huge opportunity squandered. The Indians left 9 men on base. 6 hits, 5 walks – you have to get more than 3 runs.

Game 3 – The Indians win a world series game for the first time in 47 years.

The Indians led 4-1 after 3. I felt relief. The Braves chipped away and wound up taking a 6-5 lead in the 8th. The Indians tied it in the 8th, and won in the 11th. Phew. It won't be a sweep.

Game 4 – Indians pushed to the brink.

In game 4 Steve Avery and Ken Hill traded zeros for 5 innings. Each team scored a run in the sixth. The Braves didn't stop scoring. Braves won, 5-2. The Indians again had 6 hits and 5 walks, but the Braves had 11 hits and 6 walks. It felt like the Braves were on base the entire game. Probably because they were.

Game 5 – Maddux redux.

Now we have game 5. Against Greg freaking Maddux. Bummer.

Not so fast. We have Orel Hershiser. Hershiser outpitches Maddux. Indians win, 5-4.

Five games are in the books. Every one has been a war. I haven't slept well for a week now. Kenny is sleeping like a baby. Oh wait... he is one. Games six and seven will be in Atlanta. Sleep deprivation is likely to continue for me.

Game 6 – There will be no game 7:

Going in to game 6 I felt good. We got past Maddux. Glavine looked beatable in game 2 we just didn't get to him.

I still had hope, even though it was two on games the road. It seemed like the Indians owned right handed fastball pitchers all year – so Smoltz in game 7 didn't worry me. We just had to get past Glavine.

That didn't happen. Glavine was dominant. Tony Pena got a single in the 6th. Albert Belle walked twice and Eddie Murray walked once. That was it.

In the sixth inning lefty Jim Poole came in to face David Justice. That worked out well for Justice who hit a home run. Braves win, 1-0.

I was mad at Justice for a while, but by 1997 I was over it. (Right about the time when the Indians traded Kenny Lofton and Alan Embree for Justice and Marquis Grissom.)

I actually didn't see the end of the game. My baseball buddy was running a fever. Worse – we had left our only bottle of Baby Tylenol at the babysitters.

The game ended with me in Walgreens. As happy as I was about my Tribe being in the series I didn't need to see them lose it. I saw the Browns lose to Denver in the playoffs. I saw the Cavaliers lose to the Bulls. I didn't need to see this.

1997 – A SECOND CHANCE AT THE WORLD SERIES

In 1996 the Indians won the 99 games but lost in the Divisional playoffs to Baltimore 3 games to 1. I wasn't happy that they lost to Robbie Alomar, who I didn't like. But by 1999 I liked Alomar a lot – almost as much as his brother.

The 1997 Indians finished at 86-75. That was a record that in many years wouldn't qualify for a wild card let alone a division championship (The Tribe would learn this in 2000 and again in 2005). The White Sox chased the Tribe all summer long, getting as close as 3 ½ games at the end of July.

The White Sox featured Albert Belle, my former hero but now the enemy. Belle was hated by Indians fans who felt betrayed when he signed with the White Sox for 5 years and $55 million. As the White Sox closed the gap on the Indians Belle fanned the flames by guaranteeing that the White Sox would win the division.

Apparently general manager Ken Williams didn't believe Belle. The White Sox pulled off the historic "White Flag Trade", sending starting pitchers Wilson Alvarez and Danny Darwin PLUS closer Roberto Hernandez to the San Francisco Giants for six prospects on July 31. This started a most welcome downward spiral that ended with the White Sox finishing in second, 6 games behind the Indians.

Victim number one - the New York Yankees

The Indians drew the defending champion New York Yankees in the first round. The Yankees finished 96-66, good for second place in the AL East.

I was worried about the Yankees. I didn't want to see the Indians eliminated by them. Like most Indians fans, I hate the Yankees. Which begs the question: why?

Cleveland fans hate the Yankees. I never questioned this. I grew up accepting it. Then my son asked me "Dad, why do you hate the Yankees?"

Uh… well…

I had to think about it for a while. Logically there were better choices for Indians fans' hatred. Yet it's always been the Yankees.

It's not just me. I surveyed my fellow fans when writing this book. The Yankees were "most hated" by a large margin (The Red Sox did get some mention).

(As a side note, this survey was conducted before the 2016 World Series. More on that in a bit).

SO WHY DO CLEVELAND FANS HATE THE YANKEES?

Reason 1: They took our best players and gave us squat in return.

My favorite player was Indians third baseman Graig Nettles. Nettles was great.

On November 27, 1972 the Indians traded Nettles (and catcher Gerry Moses) to the New York Yankees. The players received in return (Charley Spikes, John Ellis, Rusty Torres and Jerry Kinney) were soon forgotten. Nettles went on to hit home runs and win World Series rings with the Yankees.

Needing a new favorite player in 1973 I picked Chris Chambliss. Chambliss was the 1971 Rookie of the Year, and a great hitter. He lasted a little over a year, until:

On April 26, 1974 the Indians traded Chambliss (and pitchers Cecil Upshaw and Dick Tidrow) to the Yankees for 40% of their pitching staff

(Steve Kline, Fritz Peterson, Fred Beene, Tom Buskey). Chambliss wound up with over 2000 career hits, and World Series rings.

By the way, here's how you can tell if someone was a favorite player: If you can still remember 40 years later exactly who your team got back when the player was traded, he was a favorite.

Reason 2: They always beat us.

Since 1970, the Yankees have won 60% of the games played against the Indians.

If a team wins 60% of their games over a season that's 97 wins.

And it's not all the 1970s and 1980s when the Indians were awful.

- The Yankees were 78-50 against the Indians in the 1990s. (The decade of 2 World Series appearances and 5 divisional championships)
- The last decade where the Indians were over .500 against the Yankees AT HOME was the 1960s.
- The last decade where the Indians were over .500 against the Yankees overall? The 1910s.

It's like a Dr. Seuss book: "We will beat you here or there. We will beat you anywhere. We will beat you with a goat. We will beat you on a boat."

So it's not just a feeling. The Yankees spank the Tribe. Frequently.

Reason 3: They beat us in front of large crowds.

Growing up the Indians drew a big crowd exactly twice a year: Opening day, and Fourth of July weekend. 1976 was the bicentennial. The Independence Day to top all Independence Days. The Yankees were in Cleveland for a four game series.

Thursday, July 1 - 23,467 fans watch the Indians win 3-2.
Friday, July 2 – 35,800 fans watch Catfish Hunter beat the Tribe 7-1.
Saturday, July 3 - 64,529 fans witness Ken Holtzman beat the Tribe 7-3.
And on the bicentennial - 62,504 watch Dock Ellis beat the Tribe 4-3.

Side note: Ellis later admitted he dropped acid before pitching. I gotta believe that was one amazing bicentennial fireworks display for him

Reason 4: George Steinbrenner

But not for the reason you would think. Sure he was an obnoxious ass. He fired managers faster than Jimmy Haslem fires head coaches. 20 managers fired in 23 years. He fired Billy Martin FIVE times...

"Bring me Billy Martin back!" "Uh, Mr. Steinbrenner – you hired him 3 months ago..." "Okay, then fire him and give me Bob Lemon!"

You got the feeling that Seinfeld was actually presenting a toned down version of Steinbrenner.

But that's why Yankees fans hated him.

I hated him because he was successful, and he could have been ours.

On October 4, 1971, a group headed by Steinbrenner offered $8.5 million to buy the Tribe. There was a handshake agreement but then owner Vernon Stouffer backed out and took a $9 million offer from Nick Mileti.

Steinbrenner went on to buy the Yankees, and create the Bronx Zoo. But I would have LOVED to have the Cleveland Zoo. It might have come with rings.

UPDATE AFTER THE 2016 WORLD SERIES:

After the Yankees traded us Andrew Miller I no longer hate them quite as much.

I now hate the Cubs.

Back to our story

I was worried about the Yankees knocking out the Tribe. I was even more worried after the first game, when the Indians slapped a five run first on the Yankees, only to wind up on the short end of an 8-6 game. I remember thinking "This is exactly the kind of game we needed to win. Up by 5 in Yankee Stadium? You can't give this one back to them. We're done."

Two games later the Indians were behind 2-1 in the series, and 2-1 on the scoreboard. It was the bottom of the 8th inning. With bases empty and one out the Yankees brought in closer Mariano Rivera. I knew we tended to beat good closers, but not Mariano. It just doesn't happen.

One out later Sandy Alomar, Jr. became a Cleveland legend. He smacked a 2-0 pitch for an opposite field home run. I don't normally dance when I'm watching a game, but I did this time.

Rivera was money in the bank. Alomar had just robbed the bank.

The Indians were tied in the bottom of the 9th, but I had no doubt. Marquis Grissom singled, Bip Roberts bunted him to second, then Omar Vizquel singled off Ramiro Mendoza's glove (and past Derek Jeter). Game over.

Game Five, in Cleveland, was a 4-3 win. Young Jaret Wright won his second game of the series. On to the ALCS.

Victim number one - the Baltimore Orioles:

The Indians faced the Baltimore Orioles in the ALCS. The Orioles were 98-64. They had ace Mike Mussina (15-8, 3.20), Scott Erickson (16-7, 3.69) and Jimmy Key (16-10, 3.43). They had Cal Ripken, Robbie Alomar and Raffy Palmeiro. They were scary.

The Indians won, 4 games to 2. All four of the wins were one run thrillers.

In Game 2 Marquis Grissom hit a 3 run home run in the 8th off Armando Benitez. Indians won, 5-4.

Perhaps the most memorable game was game 3 when Jose Mesa blew a save in the top of the 9th (an ominous precursor of what was to come) but the Indians went on to win in 12 innings, when Marquis Grissom stole home.

It was a suicide squeeze, but Omar Vizquel didn't get the bunt down. In fact, he completely missed the ball. So did Oriole catcher Lenny Webster.

Webster casually jogged over to pick up the ball, letting Grissom run by untouched. Game over. Indians win 2-1.

Webster and manager Davey Johnson argued (vociferously) that the ball was fouled by Vizquel, but it wasn't. He missed. Game over.

Game 4 was another blown save for Mesa (looking back you start to see a pattern here), but the Indians won it on an Alomar single in the 9th against Armando Benitez.

Game 6 went to the Indians 1-0 when Tony Fernandez hit a solo home run in the 12th inning off... any guesses? Armando Benitez.

Back to the World Series!

After the Yankees and Orioles, I felt like the Indians were a lock against the Marlins.

Before the series started I checked the box on my dresser. It was still there. A $10 ticket from Vegas. Cleveland Indians, 8-1 to win the 1997 World Series. $80 wasn't a fortune, but it was headed my way. I could feel it.

My 1995 World Series sleeping baby was now my 1997 World Series 2-year-old buddy. We watched the games together until his bedtime.

Before each game we played the "announcer game". I would say "At first base... JIMMMMMM..."

He answered "THOMEEEEE!"

Or my favorite: "The shortstop... OMAR...."

"VIZCOW!"

Runner up favorite was his version of David Justice: Baby Justice...

Game One – Livan Hernandez pitched well, and Orel Hershiser did not. Marlins 7, Indians 4.

I thought this would be an easy win for the Indians. Hershiser had been money in the bank in the playoffs, but not in game one. I wasn't terribly upset, because it was in Florida. As long as we won our home games, we only needed one win in Florida.

But the next game didn't look promising: Kevin Brown vs. Chad Ogea.

Game Two – Chad Ogea pitched well, Kevin Brown did not. Indians 6, Marlins 1.

This surprised me in a great way. Ogea was our number four guy. Getting a win from him, on the road, was a huge bonus.

Game Three – Nobody pitched well. Marlins 14, Indians 11.

The Indians actually led 7-3 after 5. And 7-5 after 6. The game was still tied at 7 going in to the 9th inning. Then the Marlins dropped a 7 spot on the Indians. Seven runs. I wanted to throw up.

Four runs in the bottom of the ninth made the final score a little less ugly. But it was just lipstick on a pig.

Every single Indians pitcher pitched poorly. Charlie Nagy gave up 5 earned runs in 6 innings. He was the ace of the day.

Home field advantage goes back to the Marlins. I was worried.

Game Four – Jaret Wright = THE MAN. Indians 10, Marlins 3.

Just a good old fashioned butt kicking. 15 hits. A Matt Williams home run. A Manny Ramirez home run. This was one of my favorite games of the series. 3-0 after 1 inning. 6-0 after 3. It was the first time I didn't have to sit on the edge of my seat since… well… 1995.

Game Five – Orel walked a tightrope for 5, then things went south. Marlins 8, Indians 7.

Indians scored 3 in the bottom of the ninth. Alomar ended the game with a fly ball to deep right, but not deep enough. He's still legend.

The one thing I didn't want to see was the Indians down 3-2 and headed to Florida. But that was exactly what we were looking at.

Worse, we had Chad Ogea up against Kevin Brown again. I wasn't counting a repeat of game two.

Game Six – A repeat of Game Two. Indians 4, Marlins 1.

Chad Ogea – as of 2017 still the third most recent and fifth most recent starting pitcher to win a World Series game for the Indians. For trivia buffs, here are the seven most recent starting pitchers to win a WS game for the Tribe:

1. Corey Kluber, Game 4, 2016.
2. Corey Kluber, Game 1, 2016.
3. Chad Ogea, Game 6, 1997.
4. Jaret Wright, Game 4, 1997.
5. Chad Ogea, Game 2, 1997.
6. Orel Hershiser, Game 5, 1995.
7. Bob Lemon, Game 6, 1948.

The first game 7 of my life:

I felt really good about Game 7. Jaret Wright on the mound. He was 3-0 in the playoffs, 2 wins coming against the Yankees, and 1 win already in the series. My logic was: "Well, Ogea won two, no reason Wright can't do it." Wright loved the big games. We were going to take this series after all!

The Marlins started Al Leiter. He was the starting pitcher in the 14-11 win in Game 3. In 4 2/3 innings the Indians scored 7 against Leiter.

The Indians scored 2 in the third. I was thinking "That might be enough right there". Tony Fernandez got a two out single, scoring Thome and Grissom.

It was still 2-0 in 7th when Bobby Bonilla hit a solo shot. That ended the day for Wright. Lefty Paul Assenmacher closed out the 7th.

Mike Jackson got the first two outs in the 8th. Mike Hargrove then called on lefty Brian Anderson to get the last out. No problem.

On commercial break after the top of the 8th I went upstairs and laid out my shirt for work: My Cleveland Indians Bob Feller jersey. Somehow it felt right. Feller, arguably the best starting pitcher in Indians history, went to two World Series but never got a win. Our work dress code didn't allow for baseball jerseys, but dress codes be damned!

Meanwhile, despite my constant pleading with the TV, the Indians did not get an insurance run.

In the bottom of the 9th I called my brother. Back in 1995 we promised we would watch the Indians World Series win together.

I don't remember the exact conversation, but I do remember the events:

Jose Mesa came in to close it out.

Moises Alou led off with a single.

Bobby Bonilla (who already had one home run) up. I didn't feel so good.

Bonilla struck out. I felt much better.

Catcher Charles Johnson then singled, moving Alou to third. Our phone conversation suddenly included a lot of mentions of fecal matter.

Craig Counsell hit a rope that could have been extra bases and end the game. Fortunately, he hit it at Manny Ramirez. It was "only" a sac fly. Tie game. Blown save Mesa.

Jim Eisenreich ended the ninth with a ground out.

We agreed that I'd call back after the Indians scored, and we'd watch them win the World Series later that night.

I never called back.

Every Indian fan remembers the bottom of the 11th:

Bobby Bonilla hit a single.
Greg Zaun popped up the bunt attempt.
Craig Counsell hit a ground ball to Fernandez. He booted it. First and third with one out.

At this point the whole broadcast became the "Let's zoom in on Tony Fernandez". This irritated me (then and now). What's the point? Do we really need to see a close up of Tony Fernandez to know that he's not happy about missing that ball?

Jim Eisenreich was intentionally walked.

Infield in. I was freaking out.

Devon White – First pitch he hit a hard ground ball to Tony Fernandez who got the force out at home.

Two outs. I started to breathe again.

Edgar Renteria – strike one on a knee buckling Charlie Nagy curve. Then an 0-1 base hit up the middle.

Shit.

I just sat there. I watched Jim Leyland take a victory lap around Pro Player stadium. I listened to the announcers talk about how wonderful it is that Leyland finally won a World Series. And I think "Why don't you stop for another cigarette you old fart?"

Why exactly I was mad at Leyland remains a mystery. He managed the Pirates, then the Tigers. He was from Perrysburg Ohio. He was a baseball lifer, a man who made it to AA as a player then worked his way up the ranks until he managed in the big leagues. He took the Pirates to the playoffs 3 times in the early 90s, but never cracked the World Series. The Pirates then dismantled the team and Leyland was left with scrubs. He was about to endure the same fate in Florida – another fire sale was on the horizon.

In the next months I would get even madder about this series. The Indians built a team the right way. The way it should be done. With strong drafts and smart long term deals. The Marlins just opened a checkbook and gave money to veterans, all the while planning an exit strategy.

I turned off the TV, and walked upstairs. I hung the Feller jersey back up.

I laid in bed replaying the game, replaying the series in my head.

As I was about to drift off to sleep I remembered the 8 to 1 odds I got on the Indians winning the series in Las Vegas early in the year.

I got back up and tore up the ticket.

The Indians won the division in 1998 (lost the ALCS to the Yankees), 1999 (lost the ALDS to Boston) and 2001 (lost the ALDS to Seattle). After that they took a playoff break. Until 2007.

THE BOSTON MASSACRE OF 2007

Eric Wedge took over as manager of the Cleveland Indians in 2003. I remember him for two things:

Thing one I remember about Eric Wedge: His teams lost more games than the Pythagorean record said they should.

I never knew that Pythagoras took a break from triangles to analyze baseball, but apparently he did.

The Pythagorean record looks at a team's runs scored and runs yielded and says "This is how many games they should win." If you score 700 runs and give up 700 runs you should go 81-81. If you outscore your opponents by 100 you should win more than 81 games.

In 2003 the Indians run differential indicated 73 wins. They actually won 68.
In 2004 the differential said 81-81. They finished 80-82.
In 2005 it should have been 96 wins. They won 93, and missed the playoffs by one game.
2006 called for 89 wins. They managed 78.

Thing two I remember about Eric Wedge: His teams got off to slow starts:

In 2003 the Indians were bad (68-93). But in April they were awful (7-19).
In 2004 they almost hit .500 (80-82). April was 9-13.

The pieces were in place for a playoff run in 2005: Travis Hafner and Victor Martinez were beasts in the middle of the order. Young Grady Sizemore took over in center field. The rotation from 2004 (C.C. Sabathia, Jake Westbrook, Cliff Lee and Scott Elarton) got a boost with Kevin Millwood. Jhonny Peralta was taking over at shortstop.

I really hated seeing Omar Vizquel (aka Vizcow) leave, but Peralta had a promising bat. In fact, he reminded me a lot of Manny Ramirez. Especially when he got picked off first base with the bases loaded. More on that later.

The biggest problem in 2004 was the bullpen. Bob Wickman was still coming back from Tommy John surgery. The Indians tried a variety of closers in his place, most famously Jose Jiminez. Jiminez saved as many games as his ERA. That would have been fine if he only had one save, but he had 8 (along with a nifty 8.42 ERA).

It looked like the bullpen would be fixed in 2005. Wickman was healthy at closer. That meant people like Bobby Howry, Matt Miller and Rafael Betancourt could return to their normal set up roles, and Jose Jiminez could return to his normal unemployed pitcher role. Throw in newly acquired Arthur Rhodes and there was reason for hope.

I was anticipating big things. But April was another 9-14. They got hot after April. They played over .700 ball in September and October. But then there was hell week.

The Indians went into the last week of the season at 92-63. They only needed to win half of their remaining 6 games to make the playoffs. This was a team that was playing over .700 ball. Just. Win. Half. One on the road and five at home. The games were against Kansas City (on their way to a 106 loss season), Tampa Bay (headed to 95 losses) and the White Sox (who already had the playoffs clinched and could rest their starters).

How hard could it be?

The results:

Loss at KC, 5-4. Walk off win for the Royals.
Loss to Tampa Bay, 5-4.
Loss to Tampa Bay, 1-0.
Win over Tampa Bay, 6-0 – C.C. Sabathia stepped up big time.

Loss to Chicago, 3-2 in 13 innings – with an important parenting lesson thrown in.
Loss to Chicago, 4-3.
Loss to Chicago, 3-1.

The Indians finished 93-69, two games out of the playoffs.

A FAN'S LIFE - A DAD LEARNS AN IMPORTANT LESSON

In September 2005 the Indians found themselves in the thick of the wild card race, and I found myself at a campout.

Normally I prefer my critical baseball games to be closer to a TV or radio, and less in the great outdoors. But when life gets in the way I have to have a backup plan. In September 2005 the plan was for my wife and middle son to stay overnight and camp. I would take the other two boys home.

As part of my sacrifice I would get home in time for some baseball.

As I got in the car and turned on the radio, Kenny reminded me that mom promised them I would take them to Frisch's for a snack. Great. No radios there. Now what? How was I going to get home in time to listen the rest of the Indians / White Sox game? The Indians were fighting for a wild card spot!

"Do you guys want to get the food to go?"

"No, we want to eat in the restaurant."

Of course you do.

As I started the car I heard the White Sox put together 3 singles to take a 1-0 lead in the fifth. Great. Mark Buerhle was ahead 1-0.

I was so upset about the score I turned the wrong way coming out of the camp.

Of all the bad things that happened that night, turning out of the camp in the wrong direction was probably the third worst. I didn't know exactly where I was, but I knew the road from the camp would lead to the interstate in either direction. The problem was that the direction I chose took us away from home, and right toward a Frisch's.

The Frisch's I wanted was 5 minutes from home. This one was 30 minutes from home. As soon as the kids saw it, there was great rejoicing on their part.

Well, Frisch's is Frisch's. I'm going to miss the same amount of game either way.

So we stopped. Kenny got a sundae and milk, I got a hot fudge cake, and the Tommy got French fries and root beer.

When I got back in the car the score was still 1-0. It stayed that way to the bottom of the ninth. Then a Travis Hafner single followed by a Victor Martinez double and a Ronnie Belliard single tied things up.

Nothing could dampen my excitement.

The next day, as I explained the events of the night, my wife said "You didn't know that root beer made Tommy throw up?"

Apparently, there was this (unknown to me) rule that, 25 minutes after ingesting root beer, my 3-year-old son immediately emptied the contents of his stomach.

Had I known that I wouldn't have let him get Root Beer.

I sure as hell wouldn't have let him get a refill.

Did I mention that the Frisch's we ate at was 30 minutes from home? Three miles away from home, he went off like a lawn sprinkler. Suddenly his Hires Root Beer became Barq's Root Beer... then it became dad's root beer.

The game (and the car cleanup) went in to extra innings.

After I cleaned up the car I discovered that the radio in the house was not working, so I sat in the car and listened to the game. This also convinced me that a second round of air freshener was needed.

If cleaning up your son's Technicolor yawn isn't the worst thing that happened to you, that's a bad night. That was the case on this night. The White Sox put up 2 runs in the top of the 13th. The Indians responded with one in the bottom of the 13th, losing 3-2.

Back to our story:

In 2006 we had the same basic team. And they started 13-12. That's not great, but with Eric Wedge it felt like the 1927 Yankees. I figured good times were on the horizon. Nope. Final record was 78-84.

In 2007 the window of opportunity was still open. The rotation had 26-year-old C.C. Sabathia, "23" year old "Fausto Carmona", Cliff Lee, Jake Westbrook and Paul Byrd. In addition, 24-year-old Jeremy Sowers was returning after a very promising debut.

> **Fausto Carmona becomes Roberto Hernandez**
>
> On January 20, 2012 Fausto Carmona got a new name (Roberto Hernandez) and aged approximately 3 years (who knows for sure?). He was arrested in the Dominican Republic on charges of false identity.
>
> Things were going great at the security checkpoint until someone came up to him and said "Roberto? Roberto Hernandez? Hey dude, we went to high school together... Remember me???"
>
> "I have no idea who you are talking about (wink wink). I am Fausto Carmona (wink wink). I pitch for the Cleveland Indians. I couldn't have gone to school with you. I am 3 or 4 years younger than you."
>
> At which point the officer looked at Hernandez nee Carmona and said "Sir... you need to come with us..."

Sowers – who really was 24 years old - never lived up to his potential, but the rest of the rotation was very good. The bullpen was also good. Joe Borowski somehow managed to save 45 games despite a 5.07 ERA. When he blew a save, he did it right:

April 18 – Yankees score 6 in the bottom of the ninth to win 8-6.
May 13 – Oakland scores 5 in the bottom of the ninth to win 10-7. Borowski only gave up 4 of them.
August 14 – Detroit scores 4 in the top of the 10th to win 6-2.

I liked Borowski but he was in the Paul Shuey mode of pitchers – the kind of pitcher who caused me to do lots of glute exercises as I clinched my cheeks together after a walk, single, etc. on the way to a save.

The Indians' lineup featured Victor Martinez, Travis Hafner, Ryan Garko and Grady Sizemore – all with OPS over .800. Jhonny Peralta added 21 home runs.

In the middle of the year Franklin Gutiérrez (aka Goot) took over in right field. He brought a .790 OPS to the table and the range of a center fielder. A really good center fielder. On July 27 the Tribe added 40-year-old

Kenny Lofton to the outfield. That gave them the range of 3 center fielders. The outfield was a place where doubles went to die.

On August 8 the Tribe called up 21-year-old Asdrubal Cabrera, a shortstop acquired from Seattle for Eduardo Perez. Cabrera took over at second base and provided an offensive and defensive spark down the stretch.

(In 2006 the Mariners traded Cabrera for Eduardo Perez and Sin Soo Choo for Ben Broussard. Mariners GM Bill Bavasi somehow managed to NOT get fired until 2008. I'm not sure how.)

The Tigers and Indians kept trading spots in the standings. In early August the division was a tossup. Clearly the Indians couldn't afford a stupid mistake.

A stupid mistake:

The day was August 12. The Indians were trying to avoid a sweep at home (at the hands of the Yankees no less). The Indians, down 4-0, opened the bottom of the 7th inning with a Victor Martinez single, then a Ryan Garko single, then a Jhonny Peralta walk.

Peralta immediately channeled Manny Ramirez, and got picked off. With the bases loaded. And no outs.

What... the hell... was he thinking? "Hmmm... Johnny Bench, Johnny Damon, hey wait! My name is spelled differently!" Yeah, I can see that – Peralta kneeling down in the dirt, writing his name – oops! He was picked off!

The count wasn't 3-2, it was 1-0. It wasn't like they had some play on. He just had his head up his butt. Hats off to Andy Pettitte for knowing Peralta well enough to throw over and get the out. He wasn't getting any of the hitters out – might as well take the easy route.

Years later Peralta is with the St. Louis Cardinals. He holds the distinction of getting picked off first by the Cubs' Jon Lester in 2015. I didn't even know that Lester ever threw over to first.

As late as August 15 the Indians and Tigers were still tied for first. The Indians opened a lead over the next month. The Tigers came to town on September 17 for a 3 game set – still within striking distance at 4.5 games out. Three games later they were 7.5 games out, and the race was over.

For the first time in 6 years the Indians were headed to the playoffs!

Playoff opponent number one. The hated New York Yankees.

As already noted, the Yankees are just the kind of team I like to see lose. And the more embarrassing or awful way, the better.

No one will ever accuse me of being a Red Sox fan, but I did smile a little bit when the Yankees lost to the Sox after leading the series 3 games to 0.

It wasn't quite as big of a smile as the one that hit my face on August 31, 2004 when Omar Vizquel got 6 hits in a 22-0 win at Yankee stadium, but it was close.

Still, my bloodlust for awful Yankees losses was not quenched.

That's what made games one and two so satisfying.

In game 1, Chen Mien Wang started, and got beaten. Badly. The Tribe scored 3 in the first, 1 in the third and 5 in the fifth on their way to a very nice 12-3 butt whipping. Cabrera, Garko, Hafner and Martinez all did some yard work.

I couldn't imagine a better way to beat the Yankees. Then came game 2.

Game 2 was played on October 5, 2007, the ten-year anniversary of Sandy Alomar's home run off Mariano Rivera.

The Indians trailed the Yankees 1-0 in the 8th. Joba Chamberlain came in for the Yankees, and the midges came in from the lake. Midges are biting bugs that come in from Lake Erie 3 times a year or more if it's a warm October. They aren't a sweat bee, but they work the same way. They find some sweat, and bite.

Joba was sweating. And apparently yummy.

The Yankees came out and sprayed Joba, re-sprayed him, sprayed him even more with Off bug spray. This worked really well. For the Indians. It turns out that midges like Off. Avon Skin so soft supposedly works better. I'm not sure why but there was only one team using the Avon product. The home team, who gets hit with Midges 3 times a year (4 if it's a warm October) knew better.

The Indians scored 1 off Chamberlain and won 2-1 in 12 innings.

After the game George Steinbrenner complained and asked MLB to launch an investigation.

Right. Because the Indians somehow came up with a way to lure midges in from the lake. Some sort of batman type of signal. Well, maybe a midge-man type of signal.

During moments like this I wished Seinfeld was still on the air. But then again, what could they have done to make Steinbrenner look more stupid than demanding a bug swarm investigation? "Investigate those bugs Costanza! Do it now!"

The Yankees won game 3, but that was just a dead cat bouncing. The Indians, once again facing our old friend Chien Ming Wang, brought out the heavy artillery. Wang was gone in less than 2 innings, and the Yankees were gone a little over 7 innings later. Tribe 6, Yankees 4.

Playoff opponent number two. The intensely disliked (and soon to be hated almost as much as our prior opponent) Boston Red Sox:

To me it made perfect sense. Since 2000 there were no repeat World Series champions:

2000 – New York Yankees
2001 – Arizona Diamondbacks
2002 – Anaheim / California / Los Angeles / wherever Angels
2003 – Florida Marlins
2004 – Boston Red Sox (ending an 86 year drought)
2005 – Chicago White Sox (ending an 88 year drought)
2006 – St. Louis Cardinals
2007 – It must be our turn!

Game 1 – Boston strikes first.

This was an ugly start to the series. C.C. Sabathia started for the Indians and got hammered for 4+ innings. Final score: Boston 10, Cleveland 3.

Game 2 – A long game.

Game 2 went on forever. True confession time: I went to bed after 9 innings with the score tied 6-6. At the time I had a Blackberry that got a message every time a Cleveland score changed.

When I woke up the next day I noticed that I had all kinds of score updates. That had to be a good thing. If the home team wins in extra innings, you normally only get one score update.

Sure enough, the Indians piled on 7 runs in the top of the 12th inning. Tribe 13, Red Sox 6.

Game 3 – Jake Westbrook rules

Jake Westbrook was the man. Indians won 4-2. The age defying Kenny Lofton hit a home run.

Game 4 – My favorite game in the series:

The fifth inning was one of the all-time great ones:

Score tied 0-0. Tim Wakefield pitching.

Casey Blake: Solo home run. Indians 1-0.
Goot: Single.
Kelly Shoppach: Hit by pitch.
Sizemore: Fielder's choice, Shoppach out at second.
Drooby: Single off the pitcher. Goot scores. Indians 2-0.
Hafner: Strikeout swinging.
Victor Martinez: Single. Sizemore scores. Indians 3-0.
Manny Delcarmen comes in to face Jhonny Peralta.
Johnny Peralta faces Manny Delcarmen. Home run. Indians 6-0.
Kenny Lofton: Single, then a stolen base.
Casey Blake: Single. Lofton Scores. Indians 7-0.
Goot: Walk.
Shoppach: Strikes out.

The Red Sox responded in the top of the sixth with back to back to back solo homers, but it wasn't enough. Indians 7, Red Sox 3.

One game away. And we're at home. With Sabathia on the mound.

I'm pretty confident at this point. But there's a part of me that still remembers the 1999 meltdown...

The 1999 ALDS meltdown.

The 1999 ALDS got off to a wonderful start. The Indians drew Boston, which was good luck in both 1995 (3 games to 0) and 1998 (3 games to 1). The Indians ran their record to 8-1 against the Red Sox with a walk off 3-2 win followed by an 11-1 thrashing.

Game 3 – The Red Sox scored 6 runs in the bottom of the 7th to turn a 3-3 tie into a 9-3 win.

Game 4 – The Red Sox were shut out in the 6th inning only. Every other inning was a crooked number. Red Sox 23, Indians 7.

Opponents 23, Cleveland 7. That's a Browns score. (If the Browns defense has a good day.)

Game 5 – The Indians led 5-2. Then the Red Sox led 7-5. Then the Indians led 8-7. Then it was 8-8. And that was after the top of the 3rd. Enter Pedro Martinez. The Indians got no hits the rest of the way. Final: Red Sox 12, Indians 8.

The 12-8 game was Mike Hargrove's last as the Indians manager. Color me not happy.

Back to 2007:

Game 5 – I hate Josh Beckett

8 innings, 11 strikeouts, 1 run in the first and nothing more. It was close for a while, but the Red Sox pulled away late. Red Sox 7, Indians 1.

Game 6 – I hate Fausto Carmona

I felt good about game 6. We had "young" "Fausto Carmona" pitching for us.

The Red Sox treated him like old Roberto Hernandez. 10 runs in the first 3 innings. Red Sox win 12-2.

Game 7 – I hate the Red Sox

I was pleased with Jake Westbrook taking the mound for the Tribe. He won game 3. He would once again be facing Daisuke Matsuzaka. Dice K was good, but he was no Curt Schilling or Josh Beckett.

I had been bit enough times to not feel real comfortable, but I thought "We have a chance."

Early in the morning I ran the Columbus Half Marathon. I remember running by a house that had a "Go Tribe!" sign in the lawn. The homeowner was out in the yard. I yelled "We gonna take game 7 tonight?" He said "You know it."

Such optimism. In my case I was delirious from running. I have no idea what his problem was.

The turning point of the game came in the seventh inning, with the Indians down 3-2. Third base coach Joel Skinner held Kenny Lofton up at third on a single, for probably the only time in his career. Where is Jim Riggleman when we need him? (I'm fairly certain that Riggleman didn't even know what a stop sign was when he coached third).

Sure Lofton was 40, but Lofton at 40 was faster than 95% of the league, and would have scored easily.

On the other hand, there was only one out at the time, so the Indians were still fine as long as Casey Blake didn't hit into a double play.

Score Blake's at bat 5-4-3.

The Indians went with Rafael Betancourt to start the seventh. I thought this was a good move. Betancourt was money in the bank all year.

The strategy backfired. The Red Sox scored 2 in the 7th and 6 in the 8th. Game over.

That was painful, but fate had much more pain in store for me.

WHAT'S WORSE THAN LOSING IN THE PLAYOFFS?

At the time I booked the trip I couldn't have known. A trip to a late October 2007 conference in Boston. Listen to presentations at the Marriott for a couple of days, drink a few Sam Adams and eat some Legal Seafood on the company dime. What could possibly go wrong? Sign me up!

Sunday, October 28. The Red Sox are leading the Rockies in the World Series 3 games to 0. I board a plane to Manchester New Hampshire (which in Boston is pronounced Manchestah, New Hampshah. Seems that Boston natives used up all their 'er' sounds on 'ah' sounds like Philadelphier, Africer, etceterer.)

I get on and take my seat – 17C. The guy in 16C (wearing a Jason Varitek jersey) strikes up a conversation with the people seated in 17A and 17B, who are on their way back from Denver, where they attended... I can't even say it. But you know where they were. (How you can afford WS tix in Denver and still have to fly Comair through Cincinnati is beyond me.). Oh goody. They're going to talk about the game. And lucky me, the pilot said he'll provide game 4 score updates for them.

The entire flight up it's "Boston scored again" and the plane cheers.

Aren't there any mountains we can fly in to?

I figure that I'm going to get to the hotel and there will be this giant party in the bar. Fortunately, I'm wrong. Bars in Boston close early on Sunday, the entire World Series celebration was dead to me.

For a while.

Then came my birthday. Tuesday, November 1. As I'm sitting at lunch with they make an announcement: "We've had several requests to watch the Red Sox victory parade – so we're going to stream it LIVE during lunch." On a 10-foot-wide screen.

Well Happy freaking birthday to me. Can I just go up to my room and get in the fetal position and cry???

Worst birthday ever. Worst business trip ever.

2016 - THE INDIANS GET EVEN:

To this day, the Indians are my favorite of the Cleveland teams. I enjoy the slower pace of baseball. I enjoy going to a game. Between pitches I talk to my sons, father in law, or beer vendor (my father in law doubles as beer vendor sometimes).

Even if I'm watching at home I can text a friend. My grade school / high school / college friend Chris and I frequently discuss games via iMessage. I'd share the messages with you, but a lot of our best messages happened in World Series games 5 through 7.

With the Browns the discussion is generally "Who do you think they'll take with the first pick in the draft?"

And that's our September discussion.

In April I visited northern Ohio. Chris and I met for lunch. His son Tony reminded me of two things:

1) It snowed out an opening game in Cleveland this year, and
2) The last time it happened was 2007 – the year of the ALCS appearance.

This reminder would be replayed on Facebook frequently.

In May, Chris and my discussions were along this line: "This looks like a .500 team."

Then three very memorable things happened:

1. In June, after the Cavs won the NBA championship, the Indians won a club record 14 games in a row. Our discussions changed.
2. The Indians owned the Central Division. The Tribe finished 14-4 against Detroit and 14-5 against the Royals.
3. The most memorable thing happened: The 2016 playoffs.

But before we get to the playoffs – there was this great stretch in late July and August, where the Indians – normally deadline sellers, became buyers.

And they made some incredible purchases.

Purchase one – the one that got returned: Johnathan LuCroy to the Indians, Greg Allen, Francisco Mejia, Yu-Cheng Chang and Shawn Armstrong to the Brewers.

All that was needed was LuCroy to waive his right to veto the trade. He didn't.

LuCroy officially declined the trade because the Indians couldn't assure him that he would be the starting catcher in 2017, when Yan Gomes came back from his injury. He wanted his 2017 contract option voided. This would have meant that the Indians were getting exactly 1/3 the value they originally wanted. The 1970s Indians I grew up with might have been that stupid, but the 2016 Indians surely were not.

Quick note to Jonathan LuCroy on being worried that the Indians wouldn't start you at catcher in 2017: Are you kidding me? You are the best offensive catcher in baseball. You are one of, if not the best, defensive starting catchers in baseball. Were you really worried about Yan Gomes? Give us a break.

In the end, the voided trade worked out very well for the 2016 Indians. Roberto Perez did just fine for the Tribe in the World Series. And I can't help but think that we will be even happier in a few years when Allen patrols center field and Francisco Mejia is catching for the Tribe and maybe in an All Star game to boot. I don't see Chang taking over for Lindor at any point, but his bat could play at third base. Armstrong is probably in the bullpen mix for 2017 or 2018.

LuCroy was instead traded to Texas, which enabled him to start his fall vacation earlier.

The Really Big Deal: Andrew Miller to the Indians, Clint Frazier, Justis Sheffield, Ben Heller and J.P. Feyereisen to the Yankees.

The Indians gave up a lot. Frazier is now the number one prospect for the Yankees. Sheffield looks like he could be in their rotation sooner than later. Feyereisen is a strikeout machine. Heller made it to Yankee Stadium in 2016.

Doesn't matter. The Indians won this trade. Miller is the most valuable reliever in baseball. He can and will dominate at any point in the game. He turns a 9 inning game into a 7 inning game. He gives Terry Francona the ability to say at any point "Okay – the next two innings – you guys get nothing". Opponents starting to rally in the 5th? Miller Time.

The sneaky good purchase: Brandon Guyer to the Indians, Nathan Lakes to the Rays.

All Guyer did was hit .333 and record an OPS of .907. He is death on left handers. (To be fair, he doesn't have to face Andrew Miller.)

Another good buy: Coco Crisp to the Indians, Colt Hynes to the A's.

Outfielder Abraham Almonte was to be suspended for the playoffs (PEDs).

On August 31 Covelli (aka Coco) Crisp was brought in to provide a right handed bat and outfield depth. And did he ever.

Post season OPS numbers for Coco:

Boston series: .833
Toronto series: 1.025
World Series: .885

Also, he has one of the coolest names ever.

The wild ride to the World Series:

At the start of September, it looked like the Indians were in great shape for a post season run. Three weeks later? Not so much.

On September 9 Danny Salazar aggravated his elbow injury and was ruled out for an extended period. Best case, Salazar would be back for a World Series.

On September 17 Carlos Carrasco threw two pitches in Detroit. The second pitch to Ian Kinsler was lined off Carrasco's pinky finger. Broken finger – out for the season.

And I start singing "Next Year".

The Indians drew Boston in the ALDS.

A quick comparison of the rotations:

Boston:

1. Rick Porcello, Cy Young Award winner (get over it Kate Upton, your husband lost).
2. David Price
3. Clay Bucholz

Cleveland:

1. Trevor Bauer – the 5th starter if everyone is healthy.
2. Corey Kluber, pushed back a day due to a strained quad.
3. Josh Tomlin – 3 good September starts, but he was sent to the bullpen as recently as August.

Yikes.

Furthermore, the conspiracy theorist in me thinks "Big Papi is retiring. The Cubs are in the playoffs too. It will just be too good of a story – Big Papi against the Cubs. We will be eliminated. Just like 2007. And 1999."

Terry Francona had other ideas.

Game 1 – Andrew Miller dominates early.

The Red Sox lead by 1 in the bottom of the third when the Indians go all Oprah on Porcello. "You get a home run, and you get a home run and you get a home run." Roberto Perez, Jason Kipnis and Francisco Lindor all go yard.

The Red Sox close the gap to 4-3 in the fifth. That's when Tito says "Okay boys – Miller Time!" Two innings, no runs, 4 strikeouts.

Cleveland 5, Boston 4. The game ends when Dustin Pedroia thinks he checked his swing on a full count, but the umpire thinks otherwise. Strike 3, game over.

Game 2 – The Price isn't right, but Kluber surely is.

Cleveland 6, Boston 0. Corey Kluber, Dan Otero and Brian Shaw give Miller a night off.

Game 3 – Josh Tomlin gets us 5, then it's Miller Time Again.

Miller: 2 IP, 0 runs, 3K.

Cleveland 4, Boston 3.

Series over. I like Big Papi as much as the next guy. But I was glad to see him start his retirement early.

Meanwhile, Toronto swept the #1 seed Texas Rangers. This meant the Indians would have home field advantage in the ALCS.

I wanted Toronto to beat Texas, but only because of the home field advantage. Other than that, both teams looked similar to me. Lineups that would hurt you. A lot.

Game 1 – No runs for you!

Corey Kluber – 6 shutout innings.
Andrew Miller – 2 shutout innings.
Cody Allen – 1 shutout inning.

Indians 2, Blue Jays 0.

Game 2 – 1 run for you.

Josh Tomlin – 1 run in 5 innings.
Brian Shaw – 1 shutout inning.
Andrew Miller – 2 shutout innings.
Cody Allen – 1 shutout inning.

Indians 2, Blue Jays 1.

At this point, it occurs to me this is like 1995 in reverse. We are facing teams with huge scary lineups, and beating them with great pitching. Maybe not Maddux / Glavine / Smoltz great, but pretty great.

We now pause for a stupid comment by Jose Bautista.

Bautista says that circumstances are working against the Blue Jays. The Indians are getting calls to help them win, and reporters are ignoring it.

A conspiracy theory isn't necessarily stupid. I had a similar idea before the start of the Boston series.

Saying it out loud is stupid.

Game 3 – I could drone on about this…

Trevor Bauer – one of the few healthy starting pitchers – became one of the many injured starting pitchers when he cut his pinky finger while repairing a drone. 10 stitches.

On the bright side, this gave Fox a chance to zoom in on a bloody dripping finger, right up to the point where Bauer had to be removed from the game (1/3 of an inning in).

No problem. We'll just do what we did in the Carlos Carrasco finger game. Tito opens up the bullpen. Six pitchers later the Indians are looking at a sweep.

Indians 4, Blue Jays 2.

Game 4 – Okay, it won't be a sweep.

Corey Kluber gives up 2 runs, Brian Shaw and Mike Clevinger give up some more runs. Andrew Miller takes the night off.

Blue Jays 5, Indians 1.

We now pause for another stupid comment by Jose Bautista.

As the Indians prepare to send rookie Ryan Merritt to the mound (he of the one career major league start), Bautista said "He's probably shaking in his boots."

Game 5 – Shake this.

After Merritt throws 4 1/3 shutout innings the Indians light up Twitter. Trevor Bauer posts a picture of a boot with a champagne bottle in it. Corey Kluber posts a photo shopped picture of Merritt wearing Cowboy boots on the mound.

Jason Kipnis provided my favorite summary "This is why you don't say stupid shit."

Andrew Miller adds 2 2/3 more scoreless innings to his collection.

Cleveland 3, Toronto 0.

After the NBA and MLB playoffs I wonder if Toronto hates Cleveland. Probably not. We're just too nice.

As if to prove how nice Cleveland people are – some fans found Ryan Merritt's online wedding registry after game 7. The location spread through social media, and fans filled out the registry. Very cool.

Maybe we should play Toronto in football. It will never happen, because the Browns play in the NFL, and the Toronto Argonauts are in the Canadian Football League. But if it happens, my money is on Toronto.

A final note. The Indians were impressive in this series. They particularly impressed Edwin Encarnacion who signed with the Tribe in the off-season. Yes!

WORLD SERIES BABY!

The Indians prepared to do battle against the Chicago Cubs. A team that hadn't even been to the World Series since 1945. A team that hadn't won the World Series since 1908. A team that made for a great story. A team that I wanted to see lose more than anything in the world.

Game 1 – My favorite World Series game ever:

I loved the way this one started. After a couple outs Francisco Lindor gets a base hit. He then steals second base, and my kids go nuts. Free tacos from Taco Bell (steal a base steal a taco) will do that. Napoli walks. Santana walks.

Bases loaded – wow.

Jose Ramirez hits a slow roller to third. Everybody is safe. Indians 1-0. Brandon Guyer is hit by a pitch. Indians 2-0.

The inning ends when Lonnie Chisenhall fouls out.

Still, 2-0 is a nice start.

Roberto Perez handles things from there. A solo home run in the 4th, and a 3 run smash in the 8th.

Meanwhile, Kluber, Miller and Allen (sounds like a law firm) shut out the Cubs.

Indians 6, Cubs 0.

This is the first time the Indians have taken a 1 game to 0 lead in a World Series since 1920.

Kyle Schwarber – an outfielder who was recovering from a terrible knee injury in April - gets a hit in this game. Fox announcer Joe Buck immediately nominates him for World Series MVP.

Game 2 – Okay, I'll admit it… I didn't watch it

I was at an offsite meeting in Memphis, so I didn't watch it. Unless you count getting streaming updates on my phone.

The way I figured it – I could excuse myself and leave early if the game was good.

There was no need for that.

Cubs 5, Indians 1.

Schwarber goes 2 for 4. Buck nominates him for league MVP.

Game 3 – Josh Tomlin dominates

4 2/3 shutout innings. Then Miller time. Then Shaw. Then Allen. No runs for the Cubs.

Coco Crisp drives in the lone run in the 7th.

Indians 1, Cubs 0.

Schwarber pinch hits and pops out. Buck feels it's the most beautiful pop up in baseball history and asks that the ball be sent to Cooperstown.

Game 4 – Kluber, Miller and Otero?

I like Dan Otero. Great pitcher. But when the Indians close with Otero you know it's a blowout.

The Cubs take a 1-0 lead. Then Santana hit a home run. Then Kluber drives in a run! Lindor drives in Kipnis.

Chiz plates a run with a sac fly in the 6th.

Then in the seventh – local Chicago boy Jason Kipnis delivers big time. A 3 run home run.

Schwarber doesn't play. Buck notes that his beard looks particularly nice.

Okay, actually Buck spent some time praising Kipnis. What with him being from Chicago and all, he's almost like a Cub.

Indians 7, Cubs 2

I'm going nuts. The Indians can win this thing in Wrigley, or at home. We are one game away.

Then I notice the announcers are saying how the Cubs are still in good shape. They still have Lester, Arrieta and Hendricks for the next three games.

Right – it's worked so well for them so far.

Then friends – well acquaintances actually – say "Wow – this is just like the Cavs in reverse. Are you worried?"

No, I'm not. We have Tito. We have Miller. We have Kluber. It's our year.

We rained on the Big Papi retirement tour, what makes you think we won't do the same to the Cubs and the goat curse?

Game 5 – Where's that goat when we need him?

Terry Francona went with Drone Boy in game 5. I messaged Chris and we agreed – why not go with someone else? I wanted Merritt – figuring the off speed stuff would keep the Cubs off balance. He pointed out that game 6 would be off speed stuff with Tomlin. He thought maybe Clevinger, or (dare we dream?) Danny Salazar.

At any rate, Bauer starts, and for 3 innings pitches really well. The Indians lead 1-0.

Then in the 4th Kris Bryant hits a home run. Then 3 singles, a strikeout, a single and a sac fly and it's 3-1.

In the 6th Lindor drives in a run to close the gap to 3-2. Then one of my favorite little moments happens. Jon Lester steps off and catches Lindor leaning the wrong way. And he does NOTHING about it.

I mean – I know that Lester doesn't throw over – but even when it's a free out? Wow.

Sadly, Lindor is caught stealing (by the catcher) later anyway.

Aroldis Chapman pitches the 8th and 9th. I don't like him. He throws too fast.

Cubs 3, Indians 2.

Schwarber again does not play. Buck sends him a get well card.

Game 6 – ouch:

Bryant 4 for 5 with his 3rd home run.
Anthony Rizzo 3 for 5 with his 3rd home run.
Addison Russell 2 for 5 with a grand slam (and his 3rd home run)

That's a lot of hitting, but I knew this game was in trouble in the first. What should have been the third out wound up dropping between Tyler Naquin and Lonnie Chisenhall as both held up at the last minute.

It was scored a 2 RBI double for Addison Russell. This gave me ample opportunity to yell at the TV later in the night when Joe Buck kept talking about his record tying 6 RBI night. 4 were earned, but 2 were a gift.

The only good thing that came out of this game was Joe Maddon hitting the panic button. With the score 7-2 in the 7th inning the Indians got a base runner. So Maddon called on Aroldis Chapman for 1 1/3 innings.

I'm all for it. If it drops Chapman's fastball from 103 to 101 tomorrow, why not?

Cubs 7, Indians 2.

Schwarber goes 1 for 4, one of the few Cubs who didn't assault the Indians pitching staff. Buck is too busy celebrating Russell's 6 RBI night to notice.

Game 7 – The tattoo comment I made and then briefly regretted.

This is it. The game that will end a curse. Hopefully ours.

The Indians start Corey Kluber. Dexter Fowler greets him rather rudely with a home run.

Carlos Santana ties it with an RBI single in the third.

86

The Cubs add 2 in the fourth, and 2 more in the fifth.

At this point, the game is 5-1. The Indians haven't really done much. I won't give up on the game, but I also am pretty sure of the outcome. Why else would I have said the next sentence to my sons?

"You know what? If the Indians come back and win this thing, I'll get a Chief Wahoo tattoo on my left butt cheek."

Why I chose my left cheek remains a mystery to this day.

Within 10 minutes I start to question my judgment. After two quick outs Carlos Santana works Randy Hendricks for a walk. Joe Maddon continued to show his bullpen management skills by bringing in Jon Lester.

Kipnis singles in front of home plate. A bad throw by David Ross puts runners on second and third.

Lester then throws a wild pitch that bounces off David Ross. As Ross starts to get up he falls backwards. Kipnis never stops running. Ross gets to the ball and throws to Lester, but it's too late. A 2 run wild pitch.

One wild pitch, two runs, and Cleveland stadium is hopping. It's 5-3.

I turn to my sons and say "You know how 'bicep' sometimes sounds like 'butt cheek'?"

Because at age 54 apparently it's not getting my first tattoo that's the problem, it's hiding it under my pants.

This leads to a discussion between my middle son and I about where I'm going to get my Chief Wahoo tattoo. I say that the butt cheek would be a terrible place, because the tattoo would start out looking happy, but would sag over the next 10 years, and eventually look sad. He says "Yeah, but if the Indians are bad 10 years from now, it will be perfect."

By that logic, I guess should get a Browns helmet.

In the 8th inning, Lester is cruising. A ground out and a strike out. But then Ramirez gets an infield single.

If I were to rank hits that scream "Bring in a new pitcher!", an infield single would be at or near the bottom of the list.

But I'm not Joe Maddon. He immediately brings in Chapman.

This is a really good idea because Chapman was rested in game 6 when the Cubs blew the Indians out. Had Chapman not been rested – well even the great Andrew Miller was tired in Game 7.

Oh wait – Maddon used Chapman in game 6.

Okay, then it's still a great idea. If you're an Indians fan.

Chapman gives up a double to Brandon Guyer. This is not an infield hit. This is smoked. 6-4.

Rajai Davis then becomes honorary mayor of Cleveland when he sends a 2-2 pitch over the left field wall.

6-6. I'm googling tattoo artists.

Coco Crisp singles. Chapman is melting down. I am going nuts. I can see a 10 run inning. Just be patient.

Yan Gomes is not patient. He sees a bunch of pitches out of the strike zone, swings at 3, and the inning is over.

Cody Allen and Brian Shaw shut out the Cubs in the ninth.

Bottom of the ninth. I issue a pre-emptive apology to my left cheek. Chapman is still out there. This could be it!

1-2-3 inning from Chapman. Another extra inning game 7. The first one since the 1997 World Series in fact. Hopefully a happier ending.

But it won't happen for 17 minutes. We have a rain delay. Or as I like to think of it: Momentum killer.

One things start up again, Schwarber singles (Buck weeps), Bryant flies out. Rizzo is walked intentionally. Ben Zobrist, the one Cub who hasn't killed us much, doubles. Cubs score. Montero singles in another run.

8-6. Fantastic.

Bottom of the tenth. Two quick outs and it looks like the dream will die. But Guyer works a walk. He advances to second on defensive indifference. Mayor Davis singles him in.

This puts the game in Michael Martinez' hands. I like Martinez, but I can think of about 15 other guys I'd rather have up there right now.

I remember the Leyland victory lap. I'm not going through that again. I grab the remote and put my finger on the power button.

Martinez hits a slow roller to third. It's not slow enough. The throw is online. Click.

Cubs 8, Indians 7.

I was not happy about the outcome. But I love this Indians team. Even compared to the rest of the Indians playoff teams, there's somehow more to love here. It just feels like a group of regular guys playing because they love the game. I know that most of them are millionaires – but there wasn't a spoiled brat in the bunch.

In fairness I think the same could be said for the Cubs. But I still hate them.

It's a young team. And it's a young team with a new cleanup hitter Edwin Encarnacion. Hopefully he will take his invisible parrot on many trips around the bases. This is just the start of a 3 year (or more) window.

And they'll still have Terry Francona running the show.

And I'll say it right now. If they win the World Series in the next 3 years, I will NOT get a Chief Wahoo tattoo on my left butt cheek. (Maybe the bicep).

With time comes perspective. My friend Mark is from Chicago. He has been a Cubs fan for years. We talked regularly during the World Series. Both of us were complimentary toward the other's team. And both of us agreed – even before Game 7 was finished – this was one of the greatest World Series ever.

But I still hate the Cubs.

November 6 and I'm at dinner with my in-laws – and these friends of my in-laws come up to me. The guy says "Well who do you think will win?" He is, of course, referring to the upcoming presidential election.

He is decidedly NOT from the "Don't talk about politics or religion" school.

He feels strongly about politics. I feel strongly that I don't want to debate politics with people who feel strongly about politics. Or anyone else for that matter.

So I cleverly say "Well certainly not the Browns." This is meant to redirect the conversation from politics to sports.

It worked. Because the next words out of his mouth were "Wasn't that a great World Series?" And his wife joins in right away.

Oh shit.

I forgot they were from Chicago.

And even though I can be an ass, I'm apparently not a world class ass, because I did NOT say "Oh yeah. Just great. Loved seeing games 5 through 7. Because if there's one thing I love it's having my heart torn out and crapped on. Yee-haw. It was a fall classic for sure."

No, I just say nothing.

Before we go any further let me say one thing: I forgot they were Cubs fans because they don't wear Cubs gear. They don't talk about the Chicago fan experience. I have an excuse for not remembering their Cubs fan-ness.

They, on the other hand, do NOT have that excuse with me. I wear my Indians heart on my sleeve – and on my head (one of 15 hats). And around my neck (a scarf). They might not see me wearing my Indians jersey or

90

Indians t-shirt – but that would only mean I'm covering it up with my Chief Wahoo sweatshirt, or my 1995 Cleveland Indians jacket.

Back to the conversation.

Eventually I get the question that tells me that not only am I not a World Class ass, but I'm actually perhaps below average in ass-ishness.

"Did you see Bill Murray after the World Series when he was doing the interviews?"

I say nothing. But I'm thinking…

"Why the **** would I do that?"

"I've seen Bill Murray. I met Bill Murray. I shook his hand.

"I loved him in Caddyshack. He's brilliant. But did I watch him in the Cubs celebration? Uh no… call me a homer, but I don't like to sit glued to the TV when my favorite team is getting a colonoscopy." That's why I turned off the TV as soon as I was sure the throw to get Martinez was on the line. Or why I turn off the Browns shortly before kickoff.

"So no. Because as much as I loved Bill Murray in Caddyshack, there is one thing I hate even more.

"The Chicago freaking Cubs!

"If Art Modell and George Steinbrenner came back to life and created a bastard love child, and gave it to Bill Belichick to raise, I would hate that child less than I hate the Cubs. In fact…

- I hate the Cubs more than I hate kale.
- I hate the Cubs more than the Browns hate winning.
- I hate the Cubs more than Daffy Duck hates Bugs Bunny.
- I hate the Cubs more than Major Hochstedder hated Col. Hogan.
- I hate the Cubs more than Col. Hogan hated monogamy.
- I hate the Cubs more than Church Lady hates Satan.
- I hate the Cubs more than Jimmy Haslem hates paying rebates.
- I hate the Cubs more than Mr. Wonderful hates stupid people on Shark Tank.

- I hate the Cubs more than I hate liver.
- I hate the Cubs more than Jim Harbaugh hates headphones.
- I hate the Cubs more than I hate the song 'All About that Bass'.
- I hate the Cubs more than I hate the move 'To Wong Foo Thanks for Everything Julie Numar.'

"And bottom line – I would have rather watched 'To Wong Foo…' while listening to 'All About that Bass', eating a TV dinner of liver and kale than watch Bill Murray and the Cubs celebration.

"So no… I didn't watch it. And I never will. Not on a freaking boat, not with a freaking goat, not in a freaking house, not with a freaking mouse. Not freaking here or freaking there. I would not freaking watch it any-freaking-where."

But yeah, I'd probably watch it before I'd watch the Browns.

PART 3: THE BROWNS

"If it's yellow, let it mellow. If it's Brown, flush it down." - *My Grandma Tots when the cistern was running low.*

A FAN IS BORN – THE 1972 CLEVELAND BROWNS MEDIA GUIDE

I'm sure I still have the copy somewhere in the attic. The 1972 Cleveland Browns Media Guide. It was given to me by my buddy Bill Baumler – the same guy that offered me a spot on the Lenny Barker fishing trip.

Until I got the media guide I had no idea just how rich the Cleveland Browns' football tradition was. 1971 was a good year: The Browns were 9-5, but won the division. Sadly, they lost in the playoffs to the Baltimore Colts, 20-3.

After another season of Indians baseball, my attention turned to football and the media guide. I read it cover to cover.

45 years later, I remember two facts:

1. The Denver Broncos 27-0 shutout of the Browns in 1971 was the second time **in team history** that they were shut out in a regular season game. (The Browns were shut out twice in the playoffs, including the 1968 NFL Championship).
2. To that point in their history the Browns had experienced exactly **one** losing season – and that one season (5-7 in 1956) came after back to back league Championships.

As I grew up things didn't stay quite that good. The early 70s, early 80s and almost the entire 1990s were difficult. Especially 1996 through 1999 when there were no Browns.

THE MOMENT I WENT FROM CASUAL TO RABID FANDOM

I enjoyed the Browns in the 1970s. They weren't good, but they were entertaining. My dad and I loved watching Greg Pruitt elude tacklers with his tear away jersey.

But the 1980 season took my love of the Browns to a whole new level.

After losing their first two games fairly convincingly - 34-17 at New England, and 16-7 at home against Houston - the Browns won 11 of 14 to finish 11-5, winning the division.

This was the height of the "Kardiac Kids". The Kardiac Kids got their start in 1979. The Browns wound up 9-7. 12 of their games were decided by a touchdown or less. The Browns were 7-5 in those games. In 1980, they were 9-3 in close games. That made all the difference.

During the Kardiac Kids era, football became a Sunday tradition in our house. We came home from church and sat down to Sunday dinner –roast beef, mashed potatoes and gravy, green beans and percolated coffee. Dad would say a prayer and I would silently tag on "if you can see to it that Ozzie Newsome gets open a few times…".

After dinner, we changed clothes. I put on jeans and my orange "Kardiac Kids" t-shirt. Game time!

Almost all of the Browns wins that year were the same: Late in the 4th quarter, behind or perhaps tied, quarterback Brian Sipe marched the Browns down the field.

In the end, the Browns usually pulled out the victory.

We could talk about how the Browns season ended that year, and the associated heartbreak, but a friend of mine once told me "Remember – your audience is not your therapist". Suffice it to say that Browns fans still start crying at the mere mention of the words "Red Right 88"

Love the Browns? Skip this Paragraph… Red Right 88:

In the opening round of the playoffs the Browns trail the Raiders 14-12. Driving toward the open end of Browns stadium, the Browns called the play "Red Right 88". Brian Sipe was to find Ozzie Newsome in the end zone. If Newsome was covered, Sipe was to throw the ball to Lake Erie. Newsome was covered. Raiders defensive back Mike Davis was NOT in Lake Erie. He was in the end zone. He intercepted the ball. The Browns season was over, and the Raiders were on their way to a Super Bowl championship.

In the long run, the end of that season was irrelevant. It was all of the games leading up to the end that cemented the Browns in my heart. I never missed a game. One time a girl asked me if I wanted to come over and hang out on Sunday afternoon. "Will you have the Browns game on?" "No." "Can we hang out after the Browns game?" "No." Then No.

I believe that almost every sports fan has some reason, some event, some memory, that makes them a fan for life. The 1976 Miracle at Richfield did it for the Cavaliers, and the Indians helmet from Cedar Point did it for the Indians. I have asked many sports fans that same question. It's usually something like, sitting next to dad listening to a game on the radio, or grandpa taking me to my first game at the stadium.

NOT always though. I recently asked my nephew-in-law Dave: "Dave you're from Youngstown – the city is fairly well split – are you a Steelers fan, or a Browns fan?" He said "Steelers". I said "Why?" He said "My family are all Browns fans and I wanted to piss them off." But Dave is different in this regard. I'm not badmouthing Dave – except for the fact that he's a Steeler Fan. He's a Marine, stand-up guy and I'm lucky to know him.

But really… a Steelers fan?

> **Why do Browns fans hate the Steelers?**
>
> If you are a casual fan – you probably understand why Browns fans hate the Ravens. They took our team, moved them to Baltimore, and they are good almost every year. Some years they are great. They have as many Super Bowl victories since 1999 as we do winning seasons (two each). The master architect of their team is Ozzie Newsome, who was a star for us, and was a member of our front office when the team was ripped from Cleveland and moved to Baltimore.
>
> You might also understand why we hate the Patriots: Bill Belichick. And they cheat.
>
> But why the Steelers?
>
> 1. Geographic proximity. Pittsburgh is about a 2-hour drive from Cleveland.
> 2. City similarity. Both cities are blue collar cities. Cleveland is of course much better. But they are similar.
> 3. Team dis-similarity. Since the 1970s, the Steelers are one of the best franchises in football. The Browns are not. Not by a long shot.
> 4. They continually beat the snot out of us, and we don't like that. Mind you – that would be reason for Browns fans to hate almost every team… but with teams like the Bengals we can at least remember a time when we beat them. The Steelers? Not so much.
> 5. Their starting Quarterback (Ben Roethlisberger) is 20-2 against us since joining the league. Not to get ahead of the story – but he was the obvious choice for the Browns in the 2004 draft. But no… we had a better idea (see also the 2004 season)

This is what makes the Browns since 1999 years so damning to me. I can't hate them. I can't stop rooting for them. There are too many good memories from the 1980s. Sure most of them ended like a Greek tragedy at the hands of Denver, but still – what a ride!

DENVER GREEK TRAGEDY #1 - THE DRIVE

The Browns went 12-4 in 1986, the best record in franchise history, and the number of wins they get in about half a decade now. I loved this team. They had talent everywhere. Probably because they found talent everywhere: In the early rounds of the draft they found guys like Clay Matthews (1), Ozzie Newsome (1), Hanford Dixon (1), Chip Banks (1) and Webster Slaughter (2). In the mid to Late rounds of the draft they got people like Brian Brennan (4), Reggie Langhorne (7) and Earnest Byner (10). When they needed help on defense they traded for Carl Hairston and Sam Clancy. They used the supplemental draft to add home grown quarterback Bernie Kosar (traded two #1s to Buffalo for the pick – totally worth it). They raided the Canadian Football League for safety Felix Wright. They even took players from the old USFL: Kevin Mack, Mike Johnson, Gerald McNeil and Frank Minnifield.

Geez – now we get Cam Erving and Johnny Manziel.

"Oh yeah – I remember that guy". Ten Browns I forgot about before I wrote this book:

Boyce Green (led team in rushing in 1984)
Milt Morin
Calvin Hill
Robert L. Jackson (the linebacker)
Robert E. Jackson (the guard)
Dick "Bam Bam" Ambrose
Carl "Big Daddy" Hairston
Dino Hall
Tom Cousineau
Andre "Bad Moon" Rison

In the 1986 Division Playoffs, the Jets led 20-10 with a little over 4 minutes to go. No problem – touchdown, stop, field goal and win it in overtime. This was a team of destiny.

Next up: The Denver Broncos.

The Browns lead 20-13. The Broncos are 98 ½ yards away from tying the game. Time (5:49) isn't an issue, but distance surely is. Quick stop, get a punt, run out the clock or maybe ice it with a field goal, and we're headed to the Super Bowl.

I get a feeling like "This is going to happen." And by "this", I mean the Browns will go to the Super Bowl – not the start of a legend for Denver.

The stadium is going nuts. I'm at home watching on TV and I'm going nuts. 98 yards. Denver can't do it. Not on the Browns defense. Not on the Dawgs.

First down: Elway pass to Winder, 5 yards.
2nd and 5: Quick pitch to Winder, 2 yards. The Broncos face 3rd and 3. One quick stop, and we have the ball back. Just like I dreamed it.

On third down Winder runs up the middle. He doesn't get much. It looks like he made it. But they call for a measurement. I'm hoping for a few extra chain lengths, a bad spot, something. If he's short the Broncos have to punt. The measure shows that Winder made it by the length of the football. Bummer.

Fast forward to 2 minutes left. Elway has the ball on the Browns 47. He throws deep. His target is covered. I breathe a sigh of relief. In hindsight a complete pass would have worked better. Give Bernie the ball back with 2 minutes and see what we can do.

Elway is hit as he throws, but he's fine. He's had a sore ankle all day, but he's good to go. (Of course.)

2nd and 10: Elway drops back, and is sacked by Dave Puzzouli. A huge hit, and I'm doing the happy dance. It's third and forever. We're so close to Pasadena. I can taste it.

3rd and 18: The shotgun snap bounces off Steve Watson's butt and hits the ground. Elway picks up the ball, drops back about a mile, then delivers a laser to Mark Jackson for 25 yards.

How does this even happen? How does "snap the ball off a tight end's ass" turn into "first down"?

John Elway is how. I was already sick of him, and he was just getting started.

1st and 10: Elway throws the ball away to stop the clock. 1:20.
2nd and 10: The Browns only rush 3, but they break through and start chasing Elway! Of course they do. It's a screen pass. 13 yards. Broncos now have first and ten on the 15.

I'm getting a sick feeling in the pit of my stomach. It's less than one minute and counting, but only 15 yards to go. This is starting to suck.

1st and 10: Incomplete pass in the end zone, intended for Steve Watson.
2nd and 10: Elway (sore ankle and all) takes off and runs for 9. He gets out of bounds to stop the clock. 42 seconds left.
3rd and 1: Elway to Mark Jackson. Touchdown.

It comes down to a coin toss to start overtime.

After a 98-yard drive – I'm thinking that the Broncos will win the game if they win the toss.

The Broncos call heads. The coin lands on tails.

We have a chance – and a pretty good one. I know the defenses played well for most of the game – but Kosar is hot. We still could be headed to Pasadena!

1st and 10: Everyone is covered – so Kosar takes off. This is a last option for Bernie. He's not quick. He does manage to get a yard.
2nd and 9: Complete to Brennan at the 37 yard line. This was a check down. The Browns replaced Ozzie Newsome with McNeil in an effort to get some receivers deep. When they were covered, Bernie took the option to get 7 yards. Not bad.
3rd and 2: Inside handoff to Herman Fontenot. It was stuffed at the line.

Three and out. Ugh.

Jeff Gosset punts and the Broncos take over at the 25.

1st and 10: Sammy Winder – 5 yard run.
2nd and 5: Complete pass to Mobley at midfield. My vocabulary is now nothing but expletives.
1st and 10 at the Browns 48. Pitch to Winder, loss of 3.
2nd and 12: Screen pass – incomplete. Defensive end Sam Clancy - a former college basketball player - jumped up and almost brought down a rebound.
3rd and 12: Elway is flushed out. We may have him! We may have a shot yet! Nope – he throws a bullet on the run to Watson – complete at the Browns 23.

From here on it will just be torture.

1st and 10: Winder runs for 5.
2nd and 5: Winder stopped for no gain by Bob Golic, Clay Matthews and Mike Johnson.
3rd and 5: Winder just gets the ball to the middle of the field. No gain.

Well, here we go. Rich Karlis, the barefooted Broncos kicker, isn't notoriously long (career best to this point was 51 yards), but he's pretty accurate. This is a 32-yard attempt.

For the Karlis kick. I'm standing in front of the TV yelling "Miss it! Miss it!" I watch as the kick sails over the top of the left goal post. It looks like it's a foot wide left. He missed! Another chance! I throw up my hands to celebrate.

At that moment I look back at the TV and see the Broncos celebrating. It was called good.

"THEY CALLED THAT GOOD????"

In reality – and I can say this 30+ years later – the referee was in a better position to make the call than I was.

I still don't see how he messed it up.

DENVER TRAGEDY #2 - THE FUMBLE

In 1987 the Browns finished 10-5. Denver finished 10-4-1. That gave the Broncos home field advantage.

The Browns started out the playoffs by beating the Indianapolis Colts, 38-21. The Broncos crushed the Houston Oilers, 34-10.

The rematch was set up. I felt pretty good about it. The game would be played in Denver, but I felt like the Browns were the better team. They had a brutal schedule. Two of their losses were at San Francisco (13-2) and at New Orleans (12-3). I thought a game in Denver was winnable.

Besides, after last year, fate owed us one.

I felt good enough to invite friends / co-workers over to watch the game. A mix of Browns fans (Phil and my fellow BGSU grad Jeff), Bengals fans (Jon M, John L, Mark, Dave, Steve) and one Steelers fan (Dorm).

We were great friends at work and after work. We played softball on Thursday nights. In the summer we golfed on Friday nights. In the winter we bowled on Tuesdays and Fridays.

Dorm and I even managed to be partners in a Fantasy Football team. It caused some issues when I had to root for Louis Lipps, or Dorm had to root for Webster Slaughter, but the money we won helped smooth things over.

We were great friends unless we were watching sports. Sports turned fast friends into big bastards. Dave and Mark were on the same side in football (Bengals), but not college basketball. Thirty years later we still remember the time we watched Ohio State (Dave's team) play Kentucky (Mark's team) in the 1987 NCAA playoffs. In the middle of the game Dave jumped up, looked at Mark and said "F*** you and everyone you know in Kentucky!" (Ohio State won, 91-77...)

I figured if we could survive that, we could survive this championship game.

I was right, but just barely.

Somehow we figured that getting money involved would help. Before the game we threw some money together for one of those point pools. 100 squares, 25 cents a square, whoever is sitting on the final score gets 25 bucks.

The first half was a complete disaster. Elway led the Broncos to 3 consecutive touchdowns. The Browns managed one field goal. 21-3 at the half.

It's one of those rare times that the beating was so bad the Bengals fans let up. This happens on rare occasions. Like this game, or every Browns game since 1999.

The second half started much better. Elway threw an interception to Felix Wright and the Browns started on the Broncos 35.

One player later Bernie hit Reggie Langhorne for a quick score. 21-10.

We needed a stop.

On third down Elway dropped back to pass, got flushed from the pocket, ran in to his own offensive lineman, bounced off and hit Mark Jackson with a pass. Jackson broke two tackles. 70 yard touchdown. 28-10.

Are you kidding me?

Not to worry – the Browns had an Instant 80 yard drive. Just add Kosar. Two runs by Mack then passes to Byner, Langhorne and Byner - 3 perfect passes and 7 points. 28-17.

This time the Browns do get a stop, and it's time for another edition of the Bernie show!

Pass to Mack. Pass to Slaughter. Run by Mack. TD run Byner.

28-24. I'm pumped. I can see the Super Bowl ahead.

The Broncos managed a field goal. 31-24.

No problem. Bernie's streak of completions continued. This time it included a 53 yarder to Byner on 3rd and long.

And then, on 3rd and goal – Bernie found Webster Slaughter! Touchdown!

An 87 yard drive. It was our answer to "the drive".

Tie game.

After trading punts Denver takes over at the 23 with 5:14 left. Merlin Olson mentions "Isn't this about how much time he had in Cleveland last year?" Actually he had 5:47.

Shut up Father Murphy.

1st and 10: Pass complete to Nattiel at the Browns 48.

Well that sucked.

1st and 10: Winder up the middle for little gain.
2nd and 7: Elway overthrows Nattiel. He was open. We dodged a bullet. We need a hold. We really need a hold. Come on give me a hold.
3rd and 7: As Sam Clancy is about to hit Elway he completes a 27 yard pass to Nattiel. 1st and 10 at the 20.

1st and 10 from the 20: The Browns rush broke free. Mainly because that's what Elway wanted. Screen pass to Winder. Two missed tackles later Denver had a touchdown.

This wasn't good. But at least this drive was quick. Bernie still had 4 minutes left to move the Browns back down the field, and turn things around from last year. I refused to give up.

The Browns started on their own 24.

1st and 10 on the 24: Byner a 16 yard run.
1st and 10 on the 40. Byner 2 yard run.
2nd and 8: Complete to Brennan for 14 yards.
1st and 10 on the 44: Kosar to Brennan for 20 yards.

Two minute warning.

1st and 10 on the 24: Andre Townsend runs over center Gregg Rakoczy. Before the snap.

I'm feeling really good right now. 1st and 5 gives Bernie so many options. He can try to get the touchdown here (but I hope he doesn't – I don't want Elway to get the ball back). He can hand it off a couple of times, eat up some clock and still get a first down. I love 1st and 5.

Kosar handed it off to Byner, who showed great second effort and got a first down.

1st and 10 on the 13: Kosar throws to Byner, but he's out of the back of the end zone.
2nd and 10: Denver jumps offside, so the incomplete pass doesn't count. 5 yard gain.

Merlin Olson stops to mention that "Denver committed an aggressive penalty there, but they have come up with turnovers and big plays so many times in the past…" This would of course give him the ability to say (one play later) "As I just mentioned…"

Shut up Father Murphy.

2nd and 5: In fast motion, it looked like Byner scored the game tying touchdown. The second effort that had gotten so many yards sent him un-tackled to the end zone.

But the reality was he was stripped of the ball at the 2.

I held my breath as they took players off the pile. Maybe the Browns recovered.

They did not.

The Browns were able to stop the clock twice. That meant that Denver would ultimately have to punt with 13 seconds left.

At this point I look at our pool. I'm sitting on Denver 8, Cleveland 1. I announce that at least I will win the money.

Once again, I am wrong. The Broncos take a safety.

The Browns will get 8 seconds. Time for one Hail Mary. It isn't caught. If it had been caught it would have still been 30 yards too short.

I don't know who won the pool money. I just know it wasn't me.

My friends are laughing their asses off. I can only hope to someday laugh last.

For my Bengal fan friends, that someday came two years later when Joe Montana directed a Super Bowl winning drive.

As for getting even with my Steeler fan friend, I'm still waiting for that one.

A quick summary of what followed:

1988 – The Browns go through four different starting quarterbacks, and not because they sucked (like they do now). Bernie got hurt, Gary Danielson got hurt, Mike Pagel got hurt, then Bernie got hurt again. At one point their starting quarterback was Don Strock a 38 year old guy who was unemployed at the start of the season.

Sounds just like the current Browns, with one exception: **They made the playoffs.** They lost in the first round to Houston, but still – the entire season was a parade of injuries, and they wound up in the playoffs. Not bad, right? Give them a mulligan right?

Wrong. Art Modell switched coaches.

1989 – New coach Bud Carson takes the team to the conference finals against Denver. Denver wins again.

1990 – The Browns give a preview of what's to become the norm 10 years from now: 3-13.

1991 – Bill Belichick is hired.

1993 – Smilin Bill and Mike Lombardi cut Bernie Kosar in the middle of the season.

1994 – The Browns make the playoffs and lose to the Steelers. Ugh.

1995 – Art Modell earns his EZ Pass on the highway to hell when he moves the team to Baltimore.

1996 through 1998 – The Browns don't exist. This winds up being the best stretch of football in the past 20 years of the Cleveland Browns.

1999 – THE BROWNS ARE BACK – SORT OF.

I struggled with a title for this book. I figured I wanted Gold (signifying the Cavaliers winning the NBA championship as well as their color). I liked Silver for the Indians (World Series runners up). But what about the Browns?

My first idea was "Gold, Silver and Shit". But I wanted my mom to buy the book.

Additionally, I believe Amazon is worried about a defamation of character lawsuit from the shit industry.

I then decided to go with "Gold, Silver and Dung". But that sounds almost high quality compared to what the Browns have done.

Then I tried "Gold, Silver and Flop." If the Browns were a Broadway show, they would have to be considered a flop. Also, there is the somewhat less used definition of the word flop as in cow flop (aka cow shit).

Eventually I went a different direction. "Hard to Believeland". "Believeland" is a tribute to the Cavaliers and Indians, who rewarded Cleveland fans like me with a championship, and a near championship. "Hard to Believe" is for the Browns.

It was hard to believe a team could be this bad. So consistently bad, for such a long time.

If the NFL gave a "saco" trophy, it would go the Browns.

Consider:

Between the start of their history (1945) and the Modell move of the team (1996) – the Browns had 12 losing seasons.

Since the 1999 return of the Browns they have experienced **16** losing seasons.

From 1945 to 1996 the Browns were shut out in 10 regular season games, and 2 playoff games.

Since the 1999 return of the Browns they have been shut out 12 times.

On the bright side, they haven't been shut out in a playoff game since their return. Of course that's easy to do when you only play in ONE playoff game in 17 years.

Between 1945 and 1995 the Browns fired a head coach after 2 seasons or fewer exactly one time (Bud Carson, 1990).

Since the 1999 return it's happened five times. (Palmer, Mangini, Shurmer, Chudzinski and Pettine). That includes 4 in the past 8 years.

Why have the Browns been so awful? What has gone wrong? Why does saying "The Browns are being run by the Three Stooges" feel like an insult to Larry, Curly and Moe? How does a team actually wind up paying two other starting quarterbacks MORE money per passing yard than Johnny Manziel?

We could debate what has gone wrong – but one thing is clear. The Browns suck. Let's not sugar coat it. The last 17 years of Cleveland Browns football has been a crap-fest. Terrible players picked by terrible general managers and led by terrible coaches, all reporting up to the worst owners in football.

Before I go any further, let me say one thing: There are some really good players who have been stuck on these teams. Players that stood by the team, through thin and thinner. Especially a couple of players named Joe. Joe Thomas and Joe Haden – you guys deserved better.

Back to my rant.

If you haven't been paying attention – the Browns haven't started sucking recently. It's been an almost non-stop, unrelenting streak of crap-ball. Don't believe me? Look at it year by year…

1999

Team Record: 2-14
Highlight: Phil Dawson kicks a field goal as time expires to beat Pittsburgh
Lowlight: Too many to mention.
Starting QBs: Tim Couch (14 games), Ty Detmer (2)

Season summarized in a tweet: We beat the Steelers. Call the season a success.

FEBRUARY 9, 1999 – THE EXPANSION DRAFT:

The Browns were given their start by picking new players in the expansion draft. This is interesting, as the Browns are not listed as an official expansion team. The Ravens are listed as an expansion team, and the Browns are a team that took a 3 year break.

Right.

Frankly, a fairer solution might have been to make the Ravens give the Browns whoever they wanted. Players like Ray Lewis and Ed Reed. Also front office personnel such as Ozzie Newsome, instead of dolts like Phil Savage and George Kokinis.

That and public flogging for Art Modell.

The Browns were supposed to suck. It was by design. In the prior expansion (Carolina and Jacksonville) the owners gave away so much to the teams that both teams made the conference championships in the second year of their existence.

For this draft, things were changed up a little. Existing NFL teams, leery of letting the Browns have any talent whatsoever, submitted lists of five players each that the Browns could pick from.

Think about that – teams could pick any five players from their rosters. Bottom feeders. Guys that were second string on special teams. Guys with bloated contracts. Guys with fumbling problems. Guys with attitude problems. Guys that could start for the 2016 Browns.

Among those on the "Available" list: Reggie White, who announced his intention to retire, but hadn't done so officially, giving Green Bay a "Free Parking" space.

The Browns had to take at least 30 players from the list of 130, and could take as many as 42.

In general, the players on the list were so "good" that San Francisco gave the Browns TE Irv Smith and DL Roy Barker in exchange for the Browns taking Antonio Langham and his $3 million salary off their hands.

Not that there wasn't ANY talent available... Among those on the list but not selected: Quarterback Kurt Warner.

The Browns didn't pick him. They went with Scott Milanovich (Tampa Bay) instead.

If you haven't heard of Scott Milanovich that simply means that:

    a. You weren't in attendance on September 8, 1996, when he threw all 3 of his career passes (completing 2) in a 21-6 loss at Detroit.
    b. You don't follow the Toronto Argonauts (head coach since 2011).

If you haven't heard of Kurt Warner that simply means you picked up the wrong book.

APRIL 17-18, 1999 - THE COLLEGE FOOTBALL DRAFT

Since 1999 the draft has normally been the Super Bowl for Browns fans. It's spring, the weather is getting nice, and all of the teams are 0-0. And we usually get to draft early in the first round!

Coming out of the draft I have found myself with waves of optimism that carry me through to the start of preseason (or at least until the next day when something goes wrong – see also the 2014 draft).

Round 1: Tim Couch, QB

They set Couch up for "success" by trading their fourth round choice for Ty Detmer. Detmer was then signed to a 7 year contract. Couch would stay on the bench until ready. They were in no hurry. Remember that... no hurry.

I liked the pick. With the benefit of hindsight, McNabb or Culpepper would have been a better choice. But at least they didn't fall for Akili Smith.

Best pick of the draft:

Round 3: Daylon McCutcheon, DB. He started for 7 seasons.

Worst pick of the draft:

Round 2b: Rahim Abdullah, LB. Started in the first year, on the bench for year 2, out of football in year 3. There was a rumor that Abdullah once asked "Does Christmas fall on the 25th of December this year?"

Notable Free Agents (college):

Although the draft didn't go entirely well – one undrafted free agent did quite well. Phil Dawson, still kicking today (although for another team now). His name will be sprinkled throughout this book, almost exclusively in great memories. He was a throwback to the Browns of my youth.

Veteran Free Agents:

Mixed in with the draft was a series of free agent signings, including Lomas Brown at LT, Scott Rehberg at RG, Orlando Brown at RT, and center Dave Wohlabaugh. LG was given to Jim Pyne, a starter from Detroit who was the number one pick in the expansion draft.

Jamir Miller, an outside linebacker from Arizona, had tried to get "Ray Lewis money". When Arizona didn't deliver he found himself in a buyer's market. Most teams had used their cap money. The Browns landed him to a one-year deal.

Chris Spielman was acquired in a trade with Buffalo for "past considerations". (There were none). Spielman was to start at middle linebacker. Unfortunately he was injured in the third preseason game, and retired.

THE 1999 SEASON IN REVIEW

The Browns went through the pre-season, winning game four against Dallas. That meant that Cleveland's soon to be unemployed fourth string players were better than Dallas' soon to be unemployed fourth string players.

Like a fool, I thought they were ready for prime time.

WORST GAME OF THE YEAR: PITTSBURGH 43, CLEVELAND 0.

When I was a freshman my high school played a conference opponent – Hopewell Loudon high school.

We lost, 43-8.

I read the account in the paper. We had one first down – a broken play in the fourth quarter against (I'm guessing) Hopewell's third string – to move the score from 43-0 to 43-6. The only other positive play was a 2-point conversion against a defense that was already celebrating.

Seriously – we completed one pass – the broken play. Those pass yards were 2/3 of our total offense. We had more passing yardage than Hopewell – because when you rush for 350 yards you don't really need to pass.

That Monday, on the announcements I heard the following: "Congratulations to our varsity football team for a good effort against Hopewell Loudon. The final score wasn't indicative of how close the game was."

Inasmuch as the final score should have been 96-0, I guess that was true.

So – in the spirit of whitewashing established on that day, allow me to say that... the final score of the return of football to Cleveland was not as bad...

Oh forget it. The Browns got killed. The final score was: Pittsburgh 43 Cleveland 0

Sunday Night Football. A national audience was treated to:

113

The Steelers rushed for 217 yards. The Browns rushed for 9.
The Steelers threw for 247 yards. The Browns threw for 52.
The Steelers had 0 turnovers. The Browns had 4.
The Steelers were an amazing 15 of 21 on third down conversions. The Browns were 0 of 7.

On the positive side, the Browns had way more punting yardage.

Things were so bad, the Browns decided to put Tim Couch in to finish the game. Couch completed one pass – to Pittsburgh.

So let's review:

The running game was non-existent.
The rush defense was terrible.
The pass defense was terrible.
And yeah – the passing offense was terrible too.

Well, it must be the quarterback's fault. The Browns threw the "Let Tim Couch develop while Ty Detmer plays" strategy out the window and let Couch start for the rest of the season. Right up until he got injured in game 15.

THE NEXT FEW GAMES:

Tennessee 26, Browns 9
Baltimore 17, Browns 10
New England 19, Browns 7
Cincinnati 18, Browns 17. Akili Smith leads a come from behind win. (Wait… what???)
Jacksonville 24, Browns 7
St. Louis 34, Browns 3 – Hey… that Kurt Warner guy is pretty good!

OCTOBER 31, 1999 – TRICK OR TREAT FOR THE SAINTS

Tim Couch hits Kevin Johnson with a 58 yard Hail Mary as time expires in New Orleans. The Browns move to 1-7 with their first win – 21-16.

BEST GAME OF THE YEAR: REVENGE!

The Browns beat the Steelers on a game ending 39-yard field goal by Phil Dawson. Browns 16, Steelers 15. At Three Rivers Stadium. This was the second and final win of the season.

If you're going to only win 2 games – make sure one of them is the Steelers.

2000

Team Record: 3-13 Highlight: Courtney Brown records 3 sacks against the Steelers and the Browns move to 2-1. Lowlight: Every game after that for both Brown and the Browns. Starting QBs: Doug Pederson (8 games) Tim Couch (7), Spergeon Wynn (1)

Season summarized in a tweet: The ugliest stretch of Browns football ever. At least until 2016.

APRIL 15-16, 2000 - THE COLLEGE FOOTBALL DRAFT

Best pick of the draft: Dennis Northcutt (Round 2) caught 399 passes in his career. That's makes him the most prolific Browns receiver picked since 1999. But there was that whole dropped pass in the 2003 playoffs.

Most catches by a receiver drafted (1999 – present):

1. Northcutt (round 2, 2000): 399
2. Kevin Johnson (round 2, 1999): 384.

Did you ever think we'd look back at 1999 and 2000 drafts as the glory days?

Worst pick of the draft: Courtney Brown, DE - #1 overall. There was some debate – should they go with (future Pro Bowler) LaVar Arrington at LB, or Courtney Brown. They went with Brown. When he was healthy he was very good. He just wasn't healthy very often.

Runner up worst pick of the draft: Spergeon Wynn, QB (Round 6). Wynn came from that noted Quarterback factory – Southwest Texas State. He completed 49.8 percent of his passes there. This was a bad pick.

What makes it a really bad pick was two facts:

1. Tom Brady was still on the board, and
2. The Browns had INTERVIEWED Brady. But Dwight Clark was frustrated because Brady wanted to talk about "the catch". Yeah –

that's a bummer when you got some quarterback who wants to talk about football and learn.

So they took a guy who couldn't complete ½ of his passes in low Division I, and expected him to succeed in the NFL. More to the point… they used a SIXTH ROUND DRAFT PICK.

I'm not a General Manger, but isn't the idea to draft guys who you think someone else will draft if you don't? This guy had a one-way ticket to UDFA land, and the Browns rescued him. He started one game. It was historic – Jacksonville 48, Cleveland 0.

SEASON IN REVIEW:

In many respects, the 2000 season was somehow a step backwards from the 1999 inaugural campaign.

For example: The worst loss in 1999 was a 43-0 loss to Pittsburgh. In 2000, they lost to Jacksonville 48-0.

Over the course of the season, they were shut out 4 times – all in divisional games. The Bengals, 4-12 were the only division opponent who didn't blank the Browns, having to settle for a 12-3 win in Cleveland later in the season.

The worst part of it from my point of view was that the season started out with so much promise. Sure the Browns lost to Jacksonville 27-7 in game one, but things got better immediately:

BEST GAME OF THE YEAR: SEPTEMBER 10 – TAKE A KNEE FOR THE FIRST TIME!

Browns 24, Bengals 7. Tim Couch gets to run out the clock at Riverfront stadium. Couch throws for 259 yards. His game rating is 96. The Browns sack Akili Smith 7 times.

Sure it was the Bengals. And sure it was Akili Smith. But a defense that recorded 7 sacks? Wow!

ONE WEEK LATER THE OTHER BEST GAME OF THE YEAR:

A week later they beat the Steelers, 23-20. Courtney Brown records 3 sacks, including one that ended the game when time ran out before the Steelers could attempt what would have been a chip shot field goal to tie.

Things certainly were looking up. Tim Couch had a game rating of 127.9. He threw for 316 yards. Brown was a sack machine. It looked like the old days with Jacksonville and Carolina. One bad year, then playoffs in year two.

WORST GAME OF THE YEAR: ALMOST ALL OF THEM AFTER.

They scored 47 points in two games. They then scored 47 points total in the next 7 games, all losses:

Oakland 36, Browns 10
Baltimore 12, Browns 0
Arizona 29, Browns 21
Denver 44, Browns 10
Pittsburgh 22, Browns 10
Cincinnati 12, Browns 3
New York Giants 24, Browns 3

After a quick one win break against New England (19-11) the Browns finished up with five more losses, including a beat down from the Ravens (44-7) followed by a trip to Jacksonville where Spergeon Wynn did anything but win – losing 48-0.

2001

Team Record: 7-9 Highlight: The Browns sweep the Ravens Lowlight: Chicago comeback Starting QBs: Tim Couch (All 16 games!) Coaching change: Chris Palmer out, Butch Davis in.

Season summarized in a tweet: 5 game improvement – things are looking up.

APRIL 21-22, 2001 - THE COLLEGE FOOTBALL DRAFT

Worst pick: Round 1 (#3 overall): Gerard Warren, DT

The Browns brain trust decided that having another monster defensive lineman next to Courtney Brown was the way to go. And everyone in the room agreed that the best defensive lineman on the board was Richard Seymour.

Oh wait – there was one guy who didn't agree. Butch Davis.

Worse – the former coach (Chris Palmer) – was convinced that the solution to the Browns anemic attack was available in the draft – LaDamian Tomlinson.

So we had three choices: We could have stuck with Palmer and had a hall of fame running back, or Butch Davis could have listened to everyone in the room and we would have had a Pro Bowl defensive lineman.

Instead we got Big Money Warren. He wasn't terrible, but given the other options, this pick is worst.

Best pick of the draft: Round 4: Anthony Henry, DB:

As a rookie he led the NFL in interceptions with 10, including a 97 yard pick 6 against Jacksonville. After four years with the Browns he was signed as a free agent by the Cowboys where he had 2 more pick 6s.

The rest of the draft:

119

In the second round the Browns took WR Quincy Morgan. He dropped a few passes, but not as many as Braylon Edwards (by my estimation anyway). Besides, he caught a touchdown that defeated the Ravens.

In the seventh round the Browns took WR Andre King, who is still the last player to catch a pass in a Browns playoff game.

WORST GAME OF THE YEAR - NOVEMBER 4 – ONSIDE KICKS, HAIL MARYS AND PICK SIX. OH MY.

The Browns, 4-2 at the time, took on the Bears at Soldier Field.

With 1:52 left in the game, the score reads Browns 21, Bears 7. The Bears drive 80 yards, and score with 28 seconds left.

The Bears then execute an onside kick, and recover. How often does that happen? Not that often.

Then the Bears completed a Hail Mary to tie the game at the end of regulation. How often does that happen? I can think of three times anyway.

In OT, the Browns stopped the Bears. Sadly, Tim Couch, who was good all day, threw a pick six after taking over, and the Bears win, 27-21.

So the Browns lost one in an awful way. How often does that happen?

Don't answer that.

BEST GAME OF THE YEAR: SWEEP!!!

The Browns win in Baltimore on November 17, 27-17. This sweeps the season series from the Ratbirds. Baltimore makes the playoffs, but has to go on the road, and they lose in the first round. Huzzah!

The Browns also swept the season series from the Ratbirds in 2007. Good times… Good times…

2002

> Team Record: 9-7
> Highlight: We made the playoffs!
> Lowlight: Dwayne Rudd throws his helmet a tad early.
> Starting QBs: Tim Couch (14 games), Kelly Holcomb (3 games)

Season summarized in a tweet: Browns are in the playoffs!

APRIL 20-21, 2002 – THE NFL DRAFT

Worst pick - Round 1: William Green, RB. The next in a series of attempts to fix the running back position. It worked, for half a season.

This is the most inexcusable pick in the Butch Davis era. He needed a running back. He had coached a running back at Miami – Clinton Portis. He also had (allegedly) said the Browns were stressing character guys. William Green had one habit in college that might have spoken to his character: He liked pot.

Honorable mention worst pick - Round 3: Melvin Fowler, OL. He was to be the center of the future. Butch Davis liked big centers, as opposed to centers like Dave Wohlabaugh, who just got the job done.

One year later it was apparent that Fowler was NOT the center of the future.

Best pick of the draft:

In rounds 4 and 5 the Browns took a total of 3 linebackers, all of whom wound up starting in 2003. Kevin Bentley played 9 seasons as a part time starter for 3 different teams. Ben Taylor started for the Browns until his career was ruined by staph in 2006. Andra Davis was the best of the bunch, starting for the Browns, intercepting 8 passes, and recording 8 sacks. Also a ton of tackles.

AUGUST 10, 2002 – JAMIR MILLER INJURED

Following a season when he recorded 13 sacks, one interception, forced four fumbles, was named all-NFL at linebacker, and did it all without being a big douchebag like certain Pittsburgh linebackers named James Harrison that I could mention, Jamir Miller is injured.

In the first quarter of the Browns 27-15 pre-season victory over Minnesota, Miller tore his right Achilles tendon.

Miller tried to recover, but finally announced his retirement on May 16, 2003.

BEST GAME OF THE YEAR: BROWNS 24, FALCONS 16.

The Browns needed a win to make the playoffs. William Green got the job done: 178 yards rushing, including a 64 yard TD run with 3:53 to go to ice the victory.

RUNNER UP WORST GAME: SEPTEMBER 8, 2002 – STUPIDEST BROWNS LOSS EVER

Given the number of awful ways the Browns have lost; it takes something special to be the stupidest. Linebacker Dwayne Rudd gave us the special. Rudd saw Kansas City QB Trent Green on the ground, and :00 on the clock, so he took off his helmet and threw it in the air to celebrate.

Let's consider this for a second. Let's just say… that the game was indeed over. Exactly how does it make sense to throw a helmet in celebration? An NFL helmet weighs about 3 pounds. Last I checked, a helmet thrown in the air will in fact, after a period of time, come back down to earth. Given that there will be several people on the field without helmets (Dwayne Rudd, referees, Dwayne Rudd wannabees, etc.) there is a chance that a 3 pound object, coming down from above, will in fact land on an un-helmeted head. As I've often told my sons: "When the best outcome you can hope for is NOT having head trauma, you really ought to reconsider doing it…"

So if Trent Green were sacked… and the game was over… this was a bad idea.

But it was worse than that. When he hit the ground Green didn't have the ball. He threw a lateral to lineman John Tait, who ran 28 yards with the ball. I watched it. It was like a really bad ballet, done in super slow motion. A 300+ pound lineman, jogging up the field as the Browns kept trying to tackle him. Of course his run was aided by the fact that there

122

were only 10 defenders pursuing him, the eleventh opting to throw his helmet and dance. In front of a referee no less.

Since this adaptation of Swan Lake took forever, the play was still in progress when Rudd threw the helmet. Helmet throwing while a game is in progress is frowned upon to the tune of 15 yards. Since the play ended on the 25, it was only half the distance: all the way down to the 12 ½ yard line.

I immediately thought "Aw hell no... a game can't end on a defensive penalty. No way... this isn't happening..."

It was happening. Given one more play, Morten Anderson came out and split the uprights. Chiefs 40, Browns 39.

In the entire history of football – was there ever a stupider way to lose a game?

Okay – was there ever a stupider way to lose a game where Leon Lett wasn't involved?

RUNNER UP WORST GAME: SEPTEMBER 29, 2002 - MULLIGAN

Tied with the Steelers in overtime, the Browns intercept Tommy Maddox. Three plays later Phil Dawson attempts a 45-yard field goal. The kick is deflected by the Steelers.

The Steelers take over and drive to the Browns six. On second down, they attempt a field goal.

Todd Peterson's kick is blocked. Peterson picks up the ball, then gets hit and fumbles. The Steelers recover.

Since the kick never made it past the line of scrimmage, the Steelers keep the ball, and get to try again on third down. It's a rule – if you block a kick and it doesn't go past the line of scrimmage – it's a free ball. I guess the idea is to encourage half-assed kick blocks.

Naturally, the second attempt is good. Final score: Steelers 16, Browns 13.

At this point the Browns were 2-2, the two losses coming from a thrown helmet and a field goal that was blocked too well.

WORST GAME OF THE YEAR: JANUARY 6, 2003 – THE ONLY PLAYOFF APPEARANCE SINCE 1994

Playing in Pittsburgh, the Browns take a 17-7 lead into the half. They extend the lead to 24-7 in the third quarter. After trading some scores, the Browns score another TD in the 4th quarter to lead 33-21.

Let's stop for a second. The game is in Pittsburgh. Had Dwayne Rudd not thrown his helmet – this playoff game is in Cleveland. Just sayin…

So the Steelers are down by 12. Tommy Maddox, a QB who was supposed to replace John Elway in Denver (but only replaced him in the hearts of Browns fans) takes over. Maddox, who finished the day with a Steelers playoff of 367 passing yards, leads yet another TD drive.

Kelly Holcomb (who wound up with 429 yards passing) takes over again. On 3rd and 12, needing a first down to close out the game, Holcomb delivers the ball to a wide open Dennis Northcutt. The ball is on the money. If Northcutt catches it, the Browns run out the clock and win. Northcutt - 6 catches for 92 yards and 2 TDs to that point - drops the ball.

The Steelers take over and score again. They now lead 36-33. The Browns try a last ditch drive. Holcomb hits Andre King in field goal range with a few seconds left, but King can't get out of bounds.

Of all the playoff losses experienced by the Browns (and I'm including the pre 1999 version here, because we can't say "losses" for the post 1999 Browns – having only been to the playoffs this ONE TIME…) this has to be the biggest one that got away. Playing on the Steelers field… catch it and it's over. When Byner fumbled against Denver (1988), the Browns were attempting to force overtime. A win wasn't guaranteed. When Sipe threw the interception in 1980 (Red Right 88) against the Raiders – the Browns were down, and would have needed a field goal in the open end of the stadium to win – far from a guarantee on that day. When Elway drove 98 yards…

Okay maybe this was the second biggest one that got away.

2003

Team Record: 5-11
Highlight: Browns 33, Steelers 13. At Pittsburgh no less.
Lowlight: Jamaal Lewis breaks the NFL rushing record against the Browns.
Starting QBs: Tim Couch (8 games), Kelly Holcomb (8)

Season summarized in a tweet: Browns hold Jamaal Lewis to less than a mile of rushing.

APRIL 26-27, 2003 – THE NFL DRAFT

Round 1: Jeff Faine, C

Oh man I hated this pick. I figured the Browns were a playmaker away from being back in the playoffs. This pick screamed "replacing a player", and in this case it was one of my favorites – Dave Wohlabaugh.

Faine made a Pro Bowl. After the Browns traded him to New Orleans.

Worst pick - Round 2: Chaun Thompson, LB

A linebacker from West Texas A&M. A small school that won 0 games. I hated this pick too.

Thompson was good on special teams. Not exactly a win for a second round pick.

Best pick: Long snapper Ryan Pontbriand was taken in the 5th round. He made the Pro Bowl twice.

WORST GAME OF THE YEAR: SEPTEMBER 14, 2003 – BALTIMORE 33, CLEVELAND 13

On the surface, this was just another in a string of Ravens butt whippings. A 20 point margin of defeat, while bad, wasn't particularly bad in the overall series. Four times between 1999 and 2009 the Ravens defeated the Browns by **more** than 20 points.

This game is notable for one reason: Any time someone sets an all-time yardage record against you – that game goes into the Hall of Shame.

Jamaal Lewis rang up a (then) record 295 yards against the Browns on 30 carries. That's a huge task, but it became much easier after Lewis took the first handoff and ran 82 yards for a touchdown.

Lewis also had a run of 63 yards for a TD in the third quarter. This conveniently happened immediately after the Browns narrowed the game to 16-13.

A third TD run, this one for 60 yards was nullified by a holding penalty. Lewis had to settle for 48 yards on that carry.

So 193 yards on 3 carries. He had to work a little harder for the other 102 yards.

Browns coach Butch Davis noted that all three of the long runs came against the same man to man defense. Good calls coach – especially the third time when the score got close.

SECOND WORST GAME: DECEMBER 22, 2003 – JAMAAL LEWIS HELD IN CHECK

In a 35-0 loss to the Ravens, the Browns defense gives up 90 fewer yards to Jamaal Lewis than they did in their prior meeting in 2003. Sadly, the prior meeting featured a record shattering 295 day for Lewis – so the Browns "held" him to 205 this time – giving him a total of 500 yards in 2 games against the Browns. Lewis joined O.J. Simpson as the only back to twice run for 200 yards against an opponent in the same season.

Additionally, Lewis took 22 carries to get his 205 yards – an average of 9.3 yards per carry. This was a half yard improvement for the Browns defense from the prior game (30 carries, 295 yards, 9.8 YPC).

Sometimes it's the little things.

BEST GAME OF THE YEAR: LEE SUGGS RUNS WILD

The Browns visit Cincinnati on the last day of the season. The Bengals have a slight chance in the playoffs.

Rookie Lee Suggs runs for 186 yards. A 78 yard touchdown turned a 7-6 deficit into a lead before halftime. A 25 yard touchdown in the 4th quarter put the Browns ahead for good. Brett Conway kicked three field goals.

And here I thought Phil Dawson was the only kicker the Browns had from 1999 to 2012. He was, except for an injury in 2003 (Conway – 3 games) and another in 2009 (Billy Cundiff – 5 games).

And here I thought Billy Cundiff only kicked for the Browns in 2013 and 2014.

Meanwhile, the Ravens beat the Steelers, so the Bengals missed by two games.

2004

Team Record: 4-12
Highlight: Jeff Garcia leads the Browns to a season opening 20-3 win over Baltimore.
Lowlight: Jeff Garcia joins a really bad club the next week.
Starting QBs: Jeff Garcia (10 games), Luke McCown (4), Kelly Holcomb (2)
Coaching change: Davis out, Terry Robiske in (interim)

Season summarized in a tweet: Cincinnati 58, Cleveland 48. Butch Davis quits.

MARCH 9, 2004 – BROWNS SIGN JEFF GARCIA:

A run and shoot guy, he doesn't fit in to the mold of a Cleveland QB – other than the fact that he wound up marrying a Playboy Playmate, just like Tim Couch.

APRIL 24-25, 2004 – THE NFL DRAFT

Best pick, sort of - Round 1: Kellen Winslow, TE

A good pick. I liked it. But I really hated what they gave up to get it. To move up from 7th to 6th the Browns gave a second round draft choice to Detroit. Detroit apparently threatened to take Winslow. Detroit then chose wide receiver Roy Williams. Williams would have filled a need in Cleveland, and Detroit was probably bluffing.

Both Winslow and Williams made Pro Bowls.

Worse – the Browns had a golden opportunity to pick an Ohio born quarterback – Ben Roethlisberger. But that ship sailed when they signed Garcia.

Worst pick, sort of – Round 4, Luke McCown, QB:

McCown later became one of 27 (so far) QBs to start for the Browns since 1999, and one of 2 brothers to do so.

The draft was pretty good overall.

WORST GAME: SEPTEMBER 18, 2004 – YOUR RATING IS... WELL... YOU DON'T HAVE ONE...

Since the Browns return in 1999 there have been nine instances where a starting quarterback recorded a game rating of 0.0. One of those was a Cleveland Brown. If I asked you to guess who, what would you say? I mean after you said "Wait – only one???"

"Brandon Weeden?" No.
"Spergeon Wynn?" No.
"Derek Anderson?" No.
"RG3?" Only for one half, not an entire game.
"Brady Quinn? Ken Dorsey? Colt McCoy?" No, no and no.

The answer is (drumroll) Jeff Garcia.

In his second start for the Browns, Quarterback Jeff Garcia completes 8 of 27 passes for 71 yards with 3 interceptions. That is a stunning 0.0 Quarterback rating.

Garcia sets a record of sorts, becoming the first quarterback to complete at least 8 passes and still manage a goose egg.

The game was still within reach at the end. That meant this cloud had a manure lining. The Browns lost Kellen Winslow to a broken leg on an onside kick at the end of the game. The Browns recovered the kick, but lost the game. Luke McCown threw the final Hail Mary. (Garcia must have been tired.)

In going 0 for 1 McCown had a QB rating of 39.6.

BEST GAME OF THE YEAR: BROWNS 34, BENGALS 17

The Bengals pin the Browns back to their own 1. Not a problem. Jeff Garcia hits Andre Davis at the 40, and Davis outruns the secondary all the way down the field for a 99 yard TD.

2005

> Team Record: 6-10
> Highlight: Trent Dilfer throws for 336 yards in Green Bay, outduels Brett Favre. Browns win 26-24.
> Highlight 2: Rueben Droughns rushes for 1232 yards, including a 75 yard TD run against Miami that is still fun to watch.
> Lowlight: Steelers beat Browns 41-0 on Christmas Eve.
> Starting QBs: Trent Dilfer (11 games), Charlie Frye (5)
> Coaching change: Terry Robiske out, Romeo Crennel in.

Season summarized in a tweet: Rookie Josh Cribbs takes a kick back for a TD. Get used to it.

APRIL 23-24, 2005 – THE NFL DRAFT

Best and Worst pick - Round 1: Braylon Edwards, WR.

Sometimes my judgment of a player is clouded by what could be described as "small sample bias". For example – I don't normally watch Notre Dame football. So when the Browns drafted Brady Quinn I thought "What? He was terrible against Ohio State... why would they do that?" Same deal with Braylon Edwards. I thought "Bad pick. He dropped all those footballs against the Buckeyes."

Small sample bias is dangerous, because it could lead to the wrong conclusion.

In the case of Edwards and Quinn it didn't, but I guess it could have.

He's the best pick because he had one Pro Bowl year. He's the worst pick because that good year was mixed in with a lot of drops and even more jackassery. The Browns eventually got tired of him and traded him away.

Honorable mention best pick - Round 2: Brodney Pool, DB

Decent pick. He had a lot of interceptions, including a 100 yard pick six against Philadelphia in 2007.

Honorable mention worst pick - Round 3: Charlie Frye, QB

Because you know – every MAC quarterback will wind up being the next Big Ben.

Best player added (and it didn't even cost a draft pick): Josh Cribbs.

Never before or since has a Brown made kick returns so exciting. And we had Eric Metcalf.

MAY 1, 2005 – WHY DIDN'T WE JUST DRAFT EVIL KNEVIL???

Kellen Winslow Jr. suffers a near fatal motorcycle accident. He misses the entire season.

BEST GAME OF THE YEAR: BROWNS 26, PACKERS 24.

At Green Bay. Trent Dilfer throws for 336 yards. Game rating of 131.8. Brett Favre throws for 341, but also throws two picks. Browns win.

WORST GAME OF THE YEAR: STEELERS 41, BROWNS 0

Christmas Eve. In Cleveland. Who ordered the coal?

2006

> Team Record: 4-12
> Highlight: LeCharles Bentley – the top available free agent on the market – signs with the Browns.
> Lowlight: LeCharles Bentley makes it through one half of one practice before suffering a career ending injury.
> Starting QBs: Charlie Frye (13 games), Derek Anderson (3)

Season summarized in a tweet: New Pro Bowl Center. One practice later: Help wanted.

April 26-27, 2008 – THE NFL DRAFT:

Round 1 Kamerion Wimbley, LB: This was a tribute to the brilliance of GM Phil Savage. The Browns are picking 12th overall. The Ravens are picking 13th. The Browns can't really decide between Kamerion Wimbley and Haloti Ngata. They need a LB, and they need a NT. So they figure they'll teach the Ravens a lesson. They trade back one spot, and pick up an extra 6th round draft choice.

Wait a minute. Two years ago we had to give up a 2nd round pick to move up one? Now we only get a 6th round pick to move back one?

Anyway – the Ravens take Ngata. The Browns take Wimbley. Then just to show the Ravens how smart they were, the Browns take nose tackle Babatunde Oshinowo in the sixth round. Although he had the perfect nose tackle name, Oshinowo only played two games – one for the Browns in 2007 and one for the Bears in 2008.

Meanwhile, Ngata made the Pro Bowl 5 times. Wimbley wasn't bad – he had 11 sacks his rookie season (isn't that roughly the number of sacks the Browns recorded as a team in 2016?). But he went to.

Worst pick - Round 3 – Travis Wilson, WR: Lasted 6 games. Got the nickname Steely hands. Nuff said.

Best pick - Round 2 D'Qwell Jackson, MLB: The Browns traded Jeff Faine to New Orleans to move up and grab Jackson. Jackson was a great pick. Faine was no longer needed, now that the Browns had LeCharles Bentley.

Unless of course Bentley suffered some kind of freakish career ending injury in the first practice.

A LITTLE WHILE LATER – BENTLEY SUFFERED SOME KIND OF FREAKISH CAREER ENDING INJURY IN HIS FIRST PRACTICE.

The Browns sign LeCharles Bentley to a 6 year $36 million contract. He made it through part of one practice before suffering a career ending knee injury.

JUNE 12, 2006 – BIG BEN WRECKS HIS BIKE

Steelers QB Ben Roethlisberger nearly dies in a motorcycle accident.

This is the difference between the Steelers and the Browns. When a Steeler has a motorcycle wreck he still starts 15 games in that season. When a Brown has a motorcycle wreck, staph sets in and he misses a year.

WORST GAME OF THE YEAR: BENGALS 30, BROWNS 0:

At Cleveland. 72,926 people had their Thanksgiving weekend ruined. Charlie Frye completed 22 of 29 passes, but 4 were to the wrong team.

BEST GAME OF THE YEAR: BROWNS 31, CHIEFS 28:

Derek Anderson leads a 4th quarter comeback. Browns turn a 28-14 deficit in to a win in overtime.

2007

> Team Record: 10-6
> Highlight: The Phil Dawson miracle field goal forces overtime and the Browns beat the Ratbirds.
> Lowlight: Playoffs on the line – the Browns lose to the Bengals.
> Starting QBs: Derek Anderson (15 games), Charlie Frye (1).

Season summarized in a tweet: 10 wins not enough. Losses to Cincinnati and Arizona doomed us.

APRIL 28-29, 2007 – THE NFL DRAFT

Best pick – ever. Round 1a – Joe Thomas, T. A 10 time (and counting) Pro Bowler and a quality human being

Worst pick - Round 1b – Brady Quinn.

My first thought: "You mean the guy the Buckeyes destroyed in the Fiesta Bowl? Really?"

My second thought: "Well, the Packers took a free falling quarterback named Aaron Rogers and it worked out for them…"

In the last pre-season game Quinn hit Joe Jurevicius with an over the shoulder touchdown pass that had maybe a 1-inch margin for error. A perfect throw. I was convinced that Brady Quinn was the guy.

I should have stuck with my first impression.

BEST GAME OF THE YEAR: NOVEMBER 18, 2007 – NO GOOD. WAIT… IT'S GOOD!

In what was one of my favorite Browns moments, Phil Dawson's 51 yard game tying field goal against Baltimore is called No Good. The Ravens leave the field as the officials discuss the kick. The officials then correctly reverse the call to Good and the teams return to the field.

The kick looked like it bounced off the upright and back on to the field, but in fact it went through the goal post and bounced on the back of the post and back out.

The Ravens whine about it - not because the field goal wasn't good (it was) - but because field goals aren't reviewable. Sucks to be you guys, get out on the field and play in the overtime. The Browns win in overtime 33-30. This is doubly important, because it means the Ravens lost.

After the season, the NFL changed the rules to allow video reviews of field goals. This rule change was known as "The Phil Dawson Rule".

WORTS GAME OF THE YEAR (MAYBE EVER): CANCEL YOUR PLAYOFF TICKETS.

This was going to be it. This was going to be the moment where the Browns broke the playoff drought. Just one win away – and the game was at Cincinnati. 5 win 9 loss Cincinnati.

The Browns storm out to a 19-0 deficit, on their way to a 19-14 loss. Derek Anderson throws 4 interceptions.

2008

Team Record: 4-12 Highlight: Browns humiliate the Giants on Monday night. Lowlight: The Browns blow 3 double digit leads in a row Starting QBs: Derek Anderson (9 games), Ken Dorsey (2), Brady Quinn (3), Bruce Gradkowski (1)

Season summarized in a tweet: Auditions for Quarterback today at 9am. Must be ready to start at 1.

APRIL 26-27 – THE NFL DRAFT

The Browns draft actually started on April 27. I'm not sure if they even attended day one. Of course the fact that they had no picks on day one means they blew no picks on day one, which makes this one of their more successful drafts.

But we have to consider how they spent those three picks:

Worst pick - Round 1 – Was traded to Dallas for a round 1 pick in the 2007 draft. That pick was used to take Brady Quinn. Not good.

Best pick - Round 6 – Nose tackle Ahtyba Rubin. As of 2016 Rubin is still starting for the NFL – and for a real team (Seattle).

The expectations were sky high after a 10-6 season. The Browns spent most of the year crushing those expectations.

WORST GAME OF THE YEAR: SO MANY OPTIONS...

Well, there was the game in Baltimore where the Browns led 27-13, but lost 37-27. Or the game the next week, where the Browns led Denver 23-10, but lost 34-30. Or the last 6 games, where the Browns scored a total of 31 points.

I think I'll go with the last game of the season. Steelers 31, Browns 0.

BEST GAME OF THE YEAR: CLEVELAND 29, BUFFALO 27

There were only four wins in 2008, but I chose this one. Not because the Browns avoided breaking a record: Had Phil Dawson not kicked a 56-yard

137

field goal late in the 4th quarter the Browns would have been the first team in NFL history to blow a double digit lead three weeks in a row.

No – the reason this made the list is what happened afterwards. In a text battle (Soon to be ex-) GM Phil Savage tells a fan to "go root for the F-ing Bills", or "go F-ing root for the Bills", or maybe "F-ing go F-ing root for the F-ing Buffa-F-ing-lo Bills. "

This event, coupled with a really bad stretch of football, convinced owner Randy Lerner to come home from managing his English League soccer team, and fire Savage. He should have just texted him. "You're f-ing fired".

2009

> Team Record: 5-11
> Highlight: Browns finish strong, winning four in a row to close at 5-11
> Lowlight: The strong finish saves Eric Mangini's job. Temporarily
> Starting QBs: Brady Quinn (9 games), Derek Anderson (7)
> Coaching and GM Change: Crennel and Savage are out, Eric Mangini and George Kokinis are in.
> Second GM Change: Kokinis fired halfway through the season. The Walrus takes over later.

Season summarized in a tweet: A 4 game winning streak creates false optimism, saves Mangini's job.

APRIL 25-26 – THE NFL DRAFT

Best pick of the draft - Round 1 – Alex Mack, C:

One of the all-time great picks for the Browns. The Browns were supposed to pick 5th, but they traded the pick to the Jets for the 17th pick, plus the Jets second round pick, plus 3 players who didn't really amount to much.

Not content to stop there, George Kokonis dropped back to 19 (picking up a 6th round pick) and then 21 (picking up another 6th round pick).

In the end all of the extra picks and players added up to almost nothing. So it comes down to this: Would you rather have Alex Mack, or Mark Sanchez (the QB the Jets drafted 5th)?

Browns win. Handily.

Worst pick of the draft: Everything the Browns did in Round 2:

Brian Robiskie, WR:

He was a Buckeye. His dad was a former Browns coach. I wanted to like the pick. I wanted him to do well. But he didn't. And I don't like the pick.

Mohamed Massaquoi, WR:

He had one big game as the number two receiver. Then the Browns traded Braylon Edwards. No more big games for MM.

David Veikune, LB:

No idea what the Browns were thinking here. Two years, no starts, 14 games active.

Rest of the draft:

In the fourth round they took USC linebacker Kaluka Maiava. This gave them two Hawaiian linebackers in one draft. I believe that's a record.

WORST GAME: DETROIT 38, CLEVELAND 37.

Hank Poteat commits Pass Interference in end zone on a Hail Mary. Detroit gets one more play - from the one-yard line - and wins 38-37.

Let's not blame Hank for everything. There was plenty of coaching stupidity to go along with the penalty. For example: Detroit was out of time outs and the Browns had the ball left, 3rd and 5, after the 2:00 warning. Naturally, the Browns threw a pass, figuring Detroit wouldn't expect it. They certainly didn't expect it to be ***incomplete,*** which is exactly what happened.

Given the extra time, Matt Stafford moved the Lions down to Hail Mary range. Hank Poteat took it from there.

But wait! There's more! Stafford was slightly hurt on the Hail Mary play, so he had to come out for one play, as long as the Browns didn't do something stupid like call a time out with :00 left on the clock.

Even if you never heard about the game you know what happened: Browns time out, Stafford comes back in and throws his 5th TD of the game.

As a final note: This was in fact a bad call. The ball was intercepted in the front of the end zone by Abe Elam, which makes it an uncatchable ball for anyone in the back of the end zone.

BEST GAME: A RECORD SETTING DAY

Who holds the Browns team single game rushing yards record? Jim Brown? No. Leroy Kelly? No. Either of the Pruitts? No. William Green? Ha ha. Good one.

The holder is Jerome Harrison, a 5th round draft choice who took over starting running back duties in 2009, and had a 3 game run like few others in Browns history. On this day, he ran over around and through the Kansas City Chiefs for 286 yards. The Browns needed those yards, plus **two** touchdown kickoff returns by Josh Cribbs (100 and 103 yards respectively) to beat the Chiefs 41-34.

This is the second of a 4 game winning streak that takes the Browns from 1-11 to 5-11, and (sadly) saves Eric Mangini's job. Never mind the fact that the wins came against teams that were going nowhere. Never mind the fact that it took all of the above mentioned heroics to scrape by Chiefs. Never mind the fact that the offense was temporarily being built on a 5'9" overachiever (Harrison) and the "passing" of Brady Quinn. At the end of the season, newly hired Mike Holmgren and owner Randy Lerner decided they had seen enough to give Mangini another year.

Technically, it's hard to believe either had seen enough – since Holmgren wasn't with the Browns until a week after this game. Lerner, meanwhile, missed 3 of the last 4 games, (although he did leave a "good luck" text with Eric Mangini). Can't really blame him – the Browns were craptastic for the better part of the year.

2010

> Team Record: 5-11
> Highlight: The Browns humiliate the Patriots. Peyton Hillis runs for 186 yards on his way to an over 1400 yard season.
> Lowlight: Happy New Year! Steelers 41 Browns 9 on January 2.
> Starting QBs: Colt McCoy (8 games), Jake Delhomme (4), Seneca Wallace (4)

Season summarized in a tweet: We led 15 games at some point, but only led 5 at the end.

APRIL 23-24 – THE NFL DRAFT

Best pick of the draft - Round 1: Joe Haden, CB:

Awesome pick. One of the best picks ever. The only thing keeping this from being the best first round pick by the Browns since 1999 is Joe Thomas.

Maybe the Browns should just draft guys named Joe.

Runner up best pick - Round 2: T. J. Ward, S:

If you want to fix a secondary, picking Haden then Ward is a fine way to do it.

Worst pick - Round 2: Montario Hardesty, RB:

A really good back in college, but frequently hurt. The Browns hoped he had overcome his injures. He had not.

Worst pick runner up - Round 3: Shawn Lauvao, OL

Never made an impact. He did appear in a cameo, wearing a Browns uniform, on Hawaii 5-0 when they were at the Pro Bowl. That was the closest he came to the Pro Bowl.

Look – it's nice to get the Hawaiian native, but come on. Joe Thomas is the annual Browns fixture at the Pro Bowl. Put him in the show.

RUNNER UP BEST GAME OF THE YEAR: OCTOBER 24, 2010 – BROWNS PUT THE HAMMER DOWN ON THE SAINTS

In the midst of another free fall season, the Browns (1-5), go to New Orleans (4-2) and beat them up, 30-17. Linebacker David Bowens earns Defensive Player of the Week with a pair of pick sixes.

BEST GAME OF THE YEAR: NOVEMBER 8, 2010 – BROWNS PUT THE HAMMER DOWN ON NEW ENGLAND!

The final score said it all: Cleveland 34 New England 14.

A game that was so bad, NEW ENGLAND ran out the clock at the end.

Even better was the way it happened. Peyton Hillis ran over the Patriots for 184 yards. The Browns ran the ball 44 times against only 19 passes. Everyone on New England's sideline knew what was coming, and they were helpless to stop it.

Is there anything sweeter than seeing Smilin Bill, who is somewhere between the 2nd and 4th biggest douchebag in the history of the Cleveland Browns (depending on your views on Braylon Edwards and Joe Banner – Modell is forever number one) ... have to stand there and take a beating like this? The last time he took a beating like this in Cleveland was... well almost every week in 1995.

All of the sudden I felt really good about a 3-5 football team. There was still a long road ahead, but the schedule didn't look too bad. The Ravens and Steelers were both ahead of the Browns, but both were coming to Cleveland late in the season. If we can beat the Patriots, we can run the table.

For the first time in 3 years (and the last time through at least 2016) I felt really good about the Browns.

NOVEMBER 14, 2010 – WELL, SO MUCH FOR THAT.

Jets 26, Browns 20 in overtime.

WORST GAME OF THE YEAR: JANUARY 2, 2011 – STEELERS 41, BROWNS 9

A quick review of 2010 and what might have been:
1. Browns lead Buccaneers 14-10 in the 4th quarter, but lose 17-14.
2. Browns lead Chiefs 14-10 at the half, 14-13 in the 4th quarter, but lose 16-14.
3. Browns lead Ravens 17-14 in the 4th quarter, but lose 24-17.
4. Browns beat Bengals 23-20.
5. Browns lead Falcons 10-6 in the 3rd quarter, but lose 20-10.
6. Browns lead Steelers 3-0 in the 2nd quarter, but lose 28-10.
7. Browns beat Saints 30-17.
8. Browns beat Patriots 34-14.
9. Browns lead Jets 10-3 after one, lead 13-10 in the 2nd quarter, tie 20-20, then lose 26-20 in OT.
10. Browns lead Jaguars 20-17 late in the 4th quarter, lose 24-20.
11. Browns beat Panthers 24-23.
12. Browns beat Dolphins 13-10.
13. Browns lead Bills 3-0 after 1 quarter, lose 13-6.
14. Browns lead Bengals 7-0 after 1 quarter, lose 19-17.
15. Browns lead Ravens 7-0 after 1 quarter, lose 20-10.

There has **never** been a Browns team that went through an entire season without having a game where the opponents scored first and never looked back.

2010 was no exception. The Steelers scored first, second, fourth and fifth – 4 touchdowns sandwiched around a Phil Dawson 19-yard field goal. By the 4th quarter it was 41-3 before the Browns got a garbage touchdown late.

Eric Mangini was fired the next day.

2011

> Team Record: 4-12
> Highlight: Browns start out 2-1.
> Lowlight: It might have been 3-0 had they not fallen asleep on defense in the opener (see below).
> Starting QBs: Colt McCoy (13 games), Seneca Wallace (3)
> Coaching change: Eric Mangini out, Fritz Shurmer in.

Season summarized in a tweet: Fritz is better than the other guy we interviewed. Let's hire him.

APRIL 28-30 – THE NFL DRAFT

Worst pick of the draft – Phil Taylor, DT:

The Browns traded down from number 6. At the time it looked like quite a haul. In reality the Browns landed an often injured defensive tackle in 2011, and an often terrible quarterback (Brandon Weeden) in 2012. All the Falcons got in return was wide receiver Julio Jones.

Best pick of the draft - Round 2 – Jabaal Sheared, DE:

He was a great fit in the 4-3. As long as the Browns stayed in a 4-3 he was great. Of course a year later, when they went to a 3-4, he wasn't as much of a fit. Eventually he wound up in New England, where he continues to be a great fit.

BEST GAME OF THE YEAR: BROWNS 6, SEAHAWKS 3

The Browns held the Seahawks to 137 yards of total offense. And there wasn't even a blizzard.

WORST GAME OF THE YEAR: BENGALS 27, BROWNS 17

Holding on to a 17-13 lead in the fourth quarter, the Browns defense huddled up. What did they talk about? The weather? The defense they were running? No one knows.

What they DIDN'T talk about was the fact that Bengals quarterback Bruce Gradkowski had his team at the line of scrimmage. Gradkowski lobbed a 40-yard touchdown pass to A. J. Green.

I have never coached professional football. That said, I'm fairly certain that defenses that line up across from the offense at the start of a play fare better statistically than those who stay in the huddle.

Of course we probably only have one instance in NFL history where the defense tried the huddle approach – so it is a bit of a small selection bias.

2012

Team Record: 5-11
Highlight: Steelers come to Cleveland still in the playoff hunt. Browns win.
Lowlight: The first round of the draft
Starting QBs: Brandon Weeden (15 games), Thad Lewis (1)
Ownership Change: Jimmy Haslem in, Randy Lerner out.
Leadership Change: Joe Banner and Mike Lombardi in.

Season summarized in a tweet: I'm Joe Banner, and you're an idiot.

APRIL 26-27 – THE NFL DRAFT

Worst pick of the draft #1 - Round 1: Trent Richardson, RB:

An awful pick. The only thing worse than this pick was the fact that the Browns gave up a 4th round, 5th round and 6th round pick to move up one slot. The 6th round choice was Pro Bowl kicker Blair Walsh. Guess we could call this trade the Blair Walsh project. Or not.

Worst pick of the draft #2 - Round 1: Brandon Weeden, QB:

A 29-year-old quarterback in the first round.

Best pick of the draft - Round 2: Mitchell Schwartz, OT:

Started for four years, then we lost him to Kansas City.

LATE 2012 – CHANGING OF THE GUARD

Owner Jimmy Haslem puts Joe Banner in charge of all things football. This will allow him to focus on his Pilot Truck Stop business – and potentially write some rebate checks. Or not.

Banner, an egomaniac who in general shows disdain for anyone not named Joe Banner, goes about putting his stamp on the franchise. As a first move he goes out and gets a lackey GM - the likes of which hadn't been seen in the NFL since George Kokinis – Mike Lombardi. Lombardi, hated by Browns fans ever since he recommended cutting Bernie Kosar, was honing his GM skills as an NFL Analyst.

Lombardi's body of work was – surprise – awful. The only draft choices he got right in 2013 were rounds 4 and 5. He traded the 4 pick to Indianapolis for a 3 in 2014, and the 5 to Pittsburgh for a 4 in 2014.

All of his other picks were… well we'll get to that in a moment.

That said, he did do one thing right: He traded Trent Richardson for a 1 just before Indianapolis slept off a 2 week long drunk (how else do you explain it?)

The Browns named Joe Banner as CEO. Banner was from Philadelphia. Eagles fans loved him as much as Browns fans loved Lombardi. That didn't bother Banner. He knew that he was easily the smartest man in the room. If you didn't believe that, you were an idiot.

His first move was the pursuit of Chip Kelly as head coach. Kelly turned him down, saying he wanted to return to Oregon… to apparently pack his bags for Philadelphia – which was the one place on earth Kelly would never have to work for Banner again. Kelly then wore out his welcome in Philadelphia and moved on to San Francisco where he conducted an epic battle with the Browns for the first overall pick in the 2017 draft.

WORST GAME OF THE YEAR: GIANTS 41, BROWNS 27

Browns score two touchdowns in the first 5 minutes of the game. It looks like things are starting to click.

Then the Giants wake up. They close out the first half with two touchdowns and a field goal in 3 minutes.

BEST GAME OF THE YEAR: BROWNS 20, STEELERS 14

Brandon Weeden opens the scoring by throwing a pick 6 to Lawrence Timmons. From there it's all Browns. Weeden is good enough, and Trent Richardson rushes for 85 yards on 29 carries. Browns win 20-14.

Sure Big Ben was out with an injury. But a win over the Steelers is a win.

2013

Team Record: 4-12
Highlight: Brian Hoyer QBs the Browns to 3 wins in a row.
Lowlight: Hoyer's injury opens the door for Brandon Weeden's return.
Starting QBs: Jason Campbell (8 games), Brandon Weeden (5), Brian Hoyer (3).
Coaching change: Fritz Shurmer out, Rod Chudzinski is in.

Season summarized in a tweet: Let's replace Fritz with Chip. Or Chud. Whatever.

APRIL 25-27 – THE NFL DRAFT

Worst pick of the draft - Barkevious Mingo, LB:

Never worked out in Cleveland. Call him a bust. He's in New England now, and probably a future Pro Bowler.

It's a shame, because if anyone ever had a name for the Dawg pound, Mingo was it.

This was a Mike Lombardi draft. There was a lot of competition for worst pick.

Best pick of the draft, for one year – Round 2 – Josh Gordon:

It was used in the 2012 supplemental draft to grab Josh Gordon. In 2013 he had a season like no other in Browns history. 87 receptions, a league leading 1,646 yards.

Or maybe it was the worst pick of the draft – Round 2 – Josh Gordon:

Everyone knows what happened after 2013.

Any time you decide to party with Johnny Manziel, you are a bust.

Another potential worst pick of the draft – Round 4 / 5:

PHIL BARTH

Browns trade back in the draft with Miami to get Davone Bess. Then they sign him to a 3 year extension. Nine drops in 2013. And a nice twitter photo with a big fatty. And rumors that Miami knew something was going wrong. Well done, Mr. Lombardi.

BEST GAME OF THE YEAR: BROWNS 24, RAVENS 18

Jason Campbell's QB rating for the game: 116.6

WORST GAME OF THE YEAR: BENGALS 41, BROWNS 20

Let's set the stage: The Browns had already beaten the Bengals 17-6 early in the season. The overall season wasn't going well for the Browns – that's what happens when you play Brandon Weeden at Quarterback - but they were only 1.5 games out of first. Win in Cincinnati and they have the division tiebreaker wrapped up.

In the first quarter, aided by a 43 yard run by Chris Ogbonnaya, the Browns drive down to the Bengals 1. They settle for a field goal.

Three plays later Andy Dalton hits Joe Haden with a nice pass. Again the Browns don't convert it to a touchdown – but a 28 yard Billy Cundiff field goal makes it 6-0 Browns.

Two plays later Andy Dalton again completed a pass to Joe Haden. This time Haden figures "No use letting the offense convert it into another field goal – I'll just take it all the way back for a pick 6". Browns 13, Bengals 0.

Dalton decides to stop throwing to Haden, instead leading the Bengals to a 3 and out.

Just as I'm starting to think this could be our year... or at least our game... the following events happen:

1. James Harrison intercepts Jason Campbell, and drags the entire offense into the end zone. An illegal block negates the touchdown and puts the Bengals comeback on hold for about 5 seconds. Dalton finally completes a TD pass to his own team – Browns 13, Bengals 7.

150

2. The Browns go 3 and out, the Bengals block a punt, run a trick play, and eventually score a TD. Bengals 14, Browns 13.
3. The Browns punt again. The Bengals block the punt again. A Bengal (Tony Dye) recovers the punt and the Browns manage to NOT put a hand on him as he crawls around. He gets up and runs to the end zone. Bengals 21, Browns 13.
4. Chris Ogbonnaya catches a pass, runs, gets hit and fumbles. The Bengals pick up the fumble and take it in for another touchdown. Bengals 28, Browns 13.
5. With 42 seconds left in the half the Browns punt. Adam Jones returns it to the Browns 32. The Bengals wind up piling on a field goal. Bengals 31, Browns 13.

That would be a terrible game… but this all happened in one quarter.

RUNNER UP WORST GAME: BROWNS STEAL DEFEAT FROM THE JAWS OF VICTORY. PATRIOTS WIN.

The Browns go up 26-14 with 2:39 left.

Tom Brady takes 1:38 to score a TD and make it 26-21.

It's going to take an onside kick. The last time the Patriots recovered an onside kick? 1994. Bill Belichick was on the field that day, coaching the Browns.

Just to make things a little easier, the refs add a 15-yard penalty on the touchdown.

The Patriots kick off from the 50. Fozzy Whitaker dove at the ball, but didn't catch it. The Patriots did.

Brady then covered 40 yards in 30 seconds. This was assisted by a 29-yard pass interference call that according to Steve Tasker was both "terrible" and "horrible".

Patriots 27, Browns 26.

2014

Team Record: 7-9
Highlight: Hoyer leads the Browns to a 21-3 victory in Cincinnati on Thursday night, moving the team to first place with a 6-3 record
Lowlight: "With the 22nd pick in the first round the Cleveland Browns select Quarterback Johnny Manziel".
Starting QBs: Brian Hoyer (13 games), Johnny Manziel (2), Connor Shaw (1)

Season summarized in a tweet: We'll be fine as long as Alex Mack stays healthy. Oh crap.

JANUARY 23, 2014 – LET'S STOP FIRING A COACH EVERY OTHER YEAR. LET'S DO IT EVERY YEAR!

At the end of the 2013 season the Browns fire Rob Chudzinski and go on a coaching search. This involved interviewing a lot of different candidates and hearing a lot of different responses ("No", "Are you kidding me?", "Let me get back to you on that", "No hablo ingles", etc.). Eventually the Browns settle on, oops I mean find the guy they wanted all along, Buffalo defensive coordinator Mike Pettine.

I'm thinking "Didn't we score 37 against Buffalo last year?" Well, yes and no. 7 came on a Travis Benjamin punt return (he plays for the Chargers now), and another 7 came on a T.J. Ward pick 6 (he plays for the Broncos now). So we scored 23.

That said, Brandon Weeden had a QB rating of 95.3 that day, so it's not like we were hiring a modern day Buddy Ryan or anything.

Pettine, to his credit, held out for a 5th year on the contract. No coach has lasted 5 years since 1999 – so getting a little extra free money is a great idea.

MAY 8-10 – THE NFL DRAFT

Best pick of the draft: Joel Bitonio (round 2) is a near Pro Bowl guard, and Christian Kirksey (round 3) is a stud linebacker.

Worst pick in the draft: When you are so bad you bump Justin Gilbert off the "Worst pick of the draft" award, that is a terrible choice. Award goes to Johnny (two years from now I'll be out of) Football.

At the time I figured that picking Johnny Manziel was okay. Certainly picking him at 22 (same position as Brady Quinn and Brandon Weeden) has some bad mojo, but still: A guy who has improvisational skills throwing to Jordan Cameron, and whoever we picked in the second round, and Josh Gordon.

Speaking of Josh: 19 hours later EPSN broke the news story that Josh Gordon has tested positive for drugs and was facing a 1 year suspension.

Afterwards we heard all kinds of stories, all about the Manziel pick.

First we heard that the Browns had Teddy Bridgewater's name written on the pick card, but at the last minute changed it to Johnny Manziel.

If that were said about any other team people would have laughed it off. Sadly – when it was said about the Browns – people said "Yeah… I could see them doing it.".

Around pick 20 Manziel sent Quarterback coach Dowell Loggains a text saying "I wish you guys would come get me. Hurry up and draft me because I want to be there. I want to wreck this league together."

Loggains forwarded the text to Jimmy Haslem who said "Pull the trigger. We're trading up to get this guy."

This indicates that Haslem, a) was a major part of the decision and b) had never heard of a group text.

Or, if not a group next, the concept of "copy/paste" was also lost on him.

The other rumor – even better – was presented on draft night. Haslem was convinced to draft Manziel by a homeless guy. Sal Paolantonio reported that Haslam was out to dinner and "a homeless person on the street looked up at me and said 'Draft Manziel'".

Only in Cleveland.

The Browns war room includes General Manager Ray Farmer and owner Jimmy Haslem. It does not include Joe Banner. Long term, this is a good thing. Short term – not so much.

Early in the year Banner paid $100,000 for an analytics based study on the available quarterbacks in the draft. The study came back with two recommendations:

1. Best option: Teddy Bridgewater.
2. Worst option: Come on – do I even have to say it?

But by the time the draft came Banner was out and Ray Farmer was in. And a homeless guy told Jimmy Haslem to take Johnny Football. And Manziel texted Dowell Loggains. That's how you build a football team.

Looking back – I wonder why I even was optimistic for 19 hours. Manziel was picked at 22 and the first thing he did was the "show me the money" gesture. Johnny: you were picked at 22. Blake Bortles got $20.6 million. You got $8.25 million. Not bad. I would take it, but consider this: The difference between Bortles and you is more than the difference between you and the last player picked – unless of course that player is being paid NEGATIVE $4.36 million.

So if Bortles didn't do the gesture, put your hands in your pockets Johnny. Show us something first.

And what exactly did he show us? Well, pictures of him in Vegas. With a rolled up $20 bill. (One assumes it would have been $100 had he been drafted in the Bortles range).

Then… he showed us a few incomplete passes.

Then… he showed his middle finger to the Washington Redskins.

Then… he showed up late for a game after partying with Josh Gordon.

Immediately after the draft we started hearing the expression "Play like a Brown". Pettine and Farmer threw the expression around frequently.

The first time the expression was used was in reference to none other than…

Johnny Manziel

Plays like a Brown. Apparently they forgot the word "pile".

THE SEASON:

After 9 games the Browns were 6-3.
After 9 games the Browns were in first place in the AFC North.
After 9 games the Browns had more wins than any season since 2007.

After 16 games things were back to normal.

BEST GAME OF THE YEAR:

Three choices:

Game 5: Clipboard Jesus (aka Charlie Whitehurst) throws 2 TD passes and stakes the Titans to a 28-3 lead. Then Brian Hoyer and the Browns go all medieval on the Titans and win, 29-28.

Game 6: Browns 31, Steelers 10. Big Ben was unimpressive. Jordan Cameron (102 yards receiving and a TD) was very impressive.

Game 9: At Cincinnati. Browns 24, Bengals 3. 4 Bengal turnovers. The offense is looking good. I wonder who is calling the plays?

WORST GAME OF THE YEAR:

Game 15. Bengals 30, Browns 0. Johnny Manziel gets a start and looks absolutely clueless. It's as if he never looked at the playbook. Johnny's game rating: 27.3

NOVEMBER / DECEMBER 2014 – "DID YOU GET MY TEXT?"

At some point in 2014 Ray Farmer decides that it would be a good idea to text plays to offensive coordinator Mike Shanahan.

It wasn't a good idea. Not at all.

2015

Team Record: 3-13
Highlight: The win in Baltimore
Lowlight: The overtime loss to Denver (have to put that story in there)
Starting QBs: Josh McCown (8 games), Johnny Manziel (6), Austin Davis (2)

Season summarized in a tweet: Heeerrrree's Johnny! There goes Johnny!

OH THAT WAS THE PROBLEM!

In the 2014-2015 offseason the Browns commissioned a design firm to change their image.

The new image included a helmet change. The old helmet, orange with a white stripe, was replaced with a slightly brighter shade of orange.

They also changed the uniforms. The Browns can now wear orange shirts with orange pants, or – in what can only be described as an homage to the results on the field – turd brown shirts with turd brown pants.

And I thought the blood clot red uniforms the Indians wore in the 70s were bad.

Just when I start to think things might improve someday, the Browns spend money on a new color helmet.

MARCH 30, 2015 – TEXT-GATE, THE CONCLUSION

Ray Farmer is suspended for four games and the Browns are fined $250,000 for Farmer's role in Text Gate. In 2014 Farmer would text plays to Mike Shanahan, who would then call them (and watch them blow up).

Ray: Just get Madden and call your plays that way.

For me this was a head scratcher. Of all the cheating scandals in NFL history, Text Gate has to be the stupidest:

Deflategate: Tom Brady plays with deflated footballs, giving him the advantage of easier throws.

157

Spygate: The Patriots videotape New York Jets defensive coaches to steal signals, giving them an advantage of knowing what the defense would be doing.

Bountygate: The Saints put bounties on opposition players in hopes of hurting them, and getting the advantage of playing against the second string.

Textgate: The Browns GM texts plays to an offensive coordinator – a guy who knows what he's doing – giving them the DISadvantage of having less effective play calling.

In light of this, the punishment – having a bad GM for 4 less games – really did fit the crime.

By the way – Why does every scandal have to end in "Gate"? If the democratic party had been at the Holiday Inn in 1972 would we be talking about Deflate Inn? If they were at the Marriott would we be talking about Deflate-iott?

Spy-Quinta?

And what if they had been staying at a Howard Johnson?

APRIL 30-MAY 2 – THE NFL DRAFT

Best pick of the draft: I'm going to go with Duke Johnson, RB in the third round. Nose tackle Danny Shelton (1st round) could still pass him up though.

Worst pick of the draft: Cameron Erving (C, round one) or Nate Orchard (LB, round 2) would be good options for this honor. But when you are the highest drafted player to get cut and NOT offered a spot on the practice squad, and you are a 4th round pick, that's pretty bad. Award goes to Vince Mayle, who is now with the Cowboys and will probably get a ring.

TIME FOR A NEW QUARTERBACK:

The Browns allow Brian Hoyer to walk. Hoyer signs with Houston. I liked Hoyer, but I understood the decision.

Meanwhile, the Buccaneers cut Josh McCown loose. The Browns signed him to a 3-year contract. He was 1-10 with Tampa, but the year before he had a rating of 109.0 for the Bears. This was a "Hey you never know" type of deal.

Also, the Browns had leftover McCown jerseys from his brother Luke.

BEST GAME OF THE YEAR: BROWNS 33, RAVENS 30.

Ravens lead 14-3 after one quarter. Josh McCown takes over. 457 yards passing. Browns win in overtime, 33-30.

WORST GAME OF THE YEAR: A CORRESPONDING RAVENS LOWLIGHT.

The Browns line up for what would be a game winning 51-yard field goal by Travis Coons. To this point, Coons has not missed a field goal all year.

Coons doesn't have the longest leg, but he's really accurate. I figure it's probably a win, and worth a kick. After all, what's the worst thing that could happen?

Brent Urban blocks the kick and Will Hill returns it for a game winning touchdown. Ravens win 33-27.

JANUARY 3, 2016 – CALL ME BILLY

Johnny Football, ruled out because of a concussion, is spotted at a Las Vegas casino. Clever guy that he is, he posts a picture of himself with his dog at home, because you know – no one ever has a saved photo on their phone. He later adds Avon Ohio as the location. He was wearing a blond wig and a fake moustache and tells people his name is Billy. Somehow people weren't fooled.

2016

Team Record: 1-15
Highlight: The Cavs win the NBA Title.
Runner up Highlight: The Indians make it all the way to the World Series.
Football related highlight: A win over San Diego saves the Browns from really bad history.
Lowlight: Every other game. Even the pre-season games.
Starting QBs: Cody Kessler (8), Robert Griffin III (5), Josh McCown (3). In addition, Kevin Hogan, Charlie Whitehurst and Terrelle Prior all played QB for different amounts of time.
Changes: Mike Pettine out, Hue Jackson in. Ray Farmer out, Sashi Brown in charge. Paul DePodesta brought in as Chief Strategy Officer.

Season summarized in a tweet: Browns win. Star Wars Movie. Another Star Wars Movie. Browns win again.

Every year I like to play "What if?" The idea is simple. What if the Browns caught some breaks?

For example:

In 2014 the Browns were 6-3 and in first place. No really – they were. The offense was working. Then Alex Mack got hurt and the offensive line went south, as did the season. Playing the "What if Alex Mack hadn't gotten hurt?" game puts the Browns (in my mind) in the playoffs.

So let's play what if on 2016. What if everything went right?

They would have beaten Miami on a last second field goal.
They would have held the lead against Baltimore.
They would have still beaten San Diego.
And they would have not blown the last Steeler game in 100 different ways.

When 4-12 was your best possible outcome, you suck.

BEFORE THE DRAFT - THE EXODUS:

In the offseason the Browns had four free agents:

Alex Mack, C: He was gone – everyone knew it. He was gone from the moment the Browns matched Jacksonville's contract offer two years before. The Browns knew it when they drafted Erving. No amount of money would keep him in Cleveland. If I could have picked one guy to keep, it would have been Mack, but that wasn't going to happen. He even had "You can't franchise me" in his contract. Sure enough – he signed with Atlanta.

Tashaun Gipson, S: I figured he was gone. The Browns were talking about Jordan Poyer as a replacement. That's never a good sign. He signed with Jacksonville, ensuring he will continue to play no more than 16 games a year for the foreseeable future.

Travis Benjamin, WR: He graduated from a good punt returner to a good wide receiver just in time. The Browns wanted him back, but San Diego wanted him more.

Mitchell Schwartz, RT: This was the one I hoped the Browns to keep. I had no idea if he wanted to stay or not. It turned out he did want to stay, but the Browns jerked him around. So he signed with Kansas City.

In addition, the Browns let go of Johnny Manziel, linebacker Craig Robertson, linebacker Karlos Dansby and safety Donte Whitner.

APRIL 28-30 – THE DRAFT

Best pick of the draft:

It's a little early, but based on his growth over the year I'm going to go with second round choice Emanuel Ogbah. Wide receiver Corey Coleman (first round) has potential. Carl Nassib (round 3) had his moments.

Sorry, not buying it:

In round 3 Hue Jackson pushes for Southern Cal quarterback Cody Kessler. Hue says "Trust me". The pick is based on analytics. Like Kessler's completion percentage (66.8 percent) and lack of interceptions (7). It is not based on his nickname "Check down Cody".

Dak Prescott was still available at this point. Completion percentage (66.2 percent) and interceptions (5) were pretty good too. And he played in the SEC.

I'm all for analytics – but let's look at all the options next time.

That said, Kessler does not get the worst pick in the draft. He's serviceable.

Worst pick of the draft:

Wide receiver Jordan Payton (Round 5) caught 1 ball for 3 yards before being suspended for PEDs.

THE "HIGHLIGHTS"

Hard to pick which game was the worst of the year. Let's just go with a 15 way tie for first.

As for the best game of the year, not much competition there. The only competition was "Will we have a best game this year?"

Philadelphia 29, Browns 10. RG3 is hit as he goes out of bounds. Separated shoulder. Time for a new quarterback.

Baltimore 25, Browns 20. Browns score the first 3 touchdowns. Ravens take it from there.

Josh McCown suffers an injury. Time for a new quarterback. Patrick Murray suffers an injury. Time for a new kicker.

Miami 30, Browns 24 (Overtime). Cody Kessler does a good job, leading the Browns to scoring position seven times. In addition, we get a pick six from rookie Briean Boddy-Calhoun.

Unfortunately, three of those scoring position drives ended with a missed field goal. This included my favorite one, the potential game winner at the end of the fourth quarter.

My wife and I were in a waiting room. The game was on TV. I watched as the Browns sacked Ryan Tannehill and recovered a fumble on the Dolphins 27 with 20 seconds left.

A 46-yard field goal attempt. By a guy who is 3 for 5 to this point. My wife finishes up and says "Do you want to watch the end?"

"Nope – he's going to miss it and they'll lose."

And so it was.

Two days after the game Josh Gordon (who was due to come off suspension after game 4) checked in to a rehab facility. I started looking at who might be available at number 1 in the upcoming draft.

Washington 31, Browns 20

Browns led 20-17 at the start of the 4th quarter. Things went downhill from there.

New England 33, Browns 13:

Kessler is hurt – clipboard Jesus (aka Charlie Whitehurst) takes over. Following the game Charlie is cut. Patriots pile up 501 yards of total offense, the most against the Browns since September 7, 2014 (Steelers, 503 yards).

Any time you give up more than a quarter mile of offense you're going to have a tough time winning.

Tennessee 28, Browns 26

Two last minute Browns' TDs – not as close as you might think.

Cincinnati 31, Browns 17

The Bengals rush for 271 yards against the Browns. And they pass for 288. That's 559 total. What is this, a college game?

New York Jets 31, Browns 28

Browns lead 10-0.

Jets lead 31-20.
Browns score one more with 20 seconds left.

Dallas 35, Browns 10

Welcome home Zeke. Try out the end zone a couple of times.

Baltimore 28, Browns 7

Browns lead 7-6 at the half. Ravens wake up after halftime.

New York Giants 27, Browns 13

Josh McCown endures 7 sacks and throws for 322 yards. But he loses 2 fumbles, one of which is a defensive touchdown.

McCown has his moments. And he seems like a good guy. But the fumbles drive me nuts.

Cincinnati 23, Browns 10

The Bengals only get 213 yards rushing this time. The defense must be getting better.

Buffalo 33, Browns 13

Nope – the Bills rush for 280. Bills total 451 yards of offense, to join the quarter mile club.

Browns 20, Chargers 17

Sure it took a blocked field goal, then a missed field goal, but a win is a win. And the Chargers only ran for 34 yards. Of course Rivers threw for 322, but there was a pick when we needed it.

The Chargers are so upset about this game they leave San Diego at the end of the year.

Steelers Scrubs 27, Browns 24 (OT)

The Steelers were already assured of a third seed in the playoffs, so they rested many of their regulars. That said, it was the Browns, and Pittsburgh still loves to slap us around.

RG3 looked good. He looked good enough to make people think about bringing him back in 2017. But not so good that you would say "bring him back for sure". That's what we needed – more questions about quarterback.

As far as winning goes, the Browns had their chances:

Brien Brady Calhoun came within a yard of having his second pick 6 of the season, but he fumbled on the 1.
Browns drove to the 2 at the end of the 4th quarter but Isaiah Crowell fumbled.
Browns had 1st and goal at the 2 in overtime, wound up settling for a field goal.

Stupid me. I saw Browns 24, Steelers 21 in overtime and assumed it was over.

Nope – it was the opening drive overtime. Pittsburgh got one more chance and scored a TD on their drive.

On the bright side – this loss guaranteed the Browns the number one pick. Had they won the pick would have gone to San Francisco.

Was there a silver lining?

Silver lining #1: There were several players who look like keepers:

CB Jamar Taylor, picked up for a swap of 7th round choices.
CB Brien Brady Calhoun (signed as a free agent).
WR Corey Coleman (1st round)
LB Emmanuel Ogbah (2nd round)
DE Carl Nassib (3rd round)
S Derrick Kindred (4th round)
TE Seth DeValve (4th round)
OL Spencer Drango (5th round)

It's too early to write any of the picks off, outside of my favorite: 7th rounder Scooby Wright III. Scoob is now with Arizona. He had a monster

165

sophomore season in college (164 tackles, 100 solo tackles, 15 sacks and 5 forced fumbles). But mostly I liked his name. "Let's put Scooby in the dawg pound!"

Silver lining #2: No one from the management team got fired. The only thing worse than going 1-15 this year would have been a restart from the top.

The Browns did fire all defensive coaches. New defensive coordinator Gregg Williams uses a 4-3. This means yet another switch. But even that comes with silver linings.

Silver lining #4: Williams' defenses are known to hit really hard, and be aggressive. Setting aside the Bountygate scandal, this is a good thing. I get tired of watching the Steelers being the division bullies. How many times did James Harrison assault a Brown? Maybe a couple of hard hits the other direction will work wonders. It did in "A Christmas Story".

Silver lining #5: This year's defensive talent sucked. We need 5-6 new starters. If ever there was a time to switch…

Silver lining #6: The Browns traded for linebacker Jamie Collins in the middle of the season, and got him to sign an extension in January.

LOOKING AHEAD

"The future's so bright I gotta wear shades" – Timbuk 3.

"Timbuk 3 aren't Browns fans" – Phil Barth

As I write this in 2017, it's a great time to be a Cleveland sports fan. The Cavs are loaded for another championship run. As of this writing J.R. Smith is hurt. David Griffin once again to the rescue. Kyle Korver is now a Cav.

And while it's true that the Warriors added Kevin Durant in the offseason, it's also true that there's only one basketball to go around to all the shooters.

I'd say a third Cavs vs. Warriors final could be on the horizon. I like our odds. (I don't love them, but I like them).

This isn't a one-year window for the Cavs either. Kyrie Irving has been around a long time – but he's only 24. Tristan Thompson is 25. Kevin Love is 28. LeBron is ageless.

The Indians are the favorite to win the AL Central, if not the entire American League. Almost everyone is coming back. One exception is Mike Napoli. The party will move to Edwin's. The Indians inked Edwin Encarnacion to a 3-year deal in the offseason. I liked Napoli – a lot. But when you can get a guy that averages 39 home runs a year, you have to take that.

More importantly, it looks like the rest of the division is going to either rebuild or struggle. The Tigers look like they are going to make another run. But they are getting older. The Royals keep losing a piece of their team here and there. The White Sox made a couple of white flag trades in the offseason. They will be good in a couple of years, but not now. The Twins have a lot of young talent, but it hasn't gotten them anywhere yet.

The Browns have a new way of doing things. And a lot of draft picks. And a couple of coaches that didn't get fired in the offseason. And Jamie Collins. It might just work out eventually.

Meanwhile, I'll continue to have a nice yard every fall.

Even if we don't score a championship in 2017 we will have the memory of 2016. The memory of a magical stretch in June when the Cavaliers went from eliminated to the eliminators, when the Indians went from a good team to a machine that won 14 games in a row and won the division easily. Those memories are what will keep us believing.

Win or lose I will still love my teams. I live 5 hours from Cleveland now, but thanks to social media I can discuss games with my friends from grade school and college. We can share the golden moments, the oh so close silver moments, and we can complain about the Browns. You can't ask for more than that.

ABOUT THE AUTHOR

Phil Barth has been a Cleveland fan from the June 1970 day he put the ill-fitting plastic Cleveland Indians "batting" helmet on his head. He survived The Drive, The Fumble, The Shot, The Decision, Jose Mesa and Red Right 88. In 2016 he enjoyed The Chasedown, The (Kyrie) Shot, and the first 4 games of the World Series. His collection of Cleveland autographs includes not only Lou Groza, Jim Thome and Zydrunas Ilgauskas, but also Jim Norris, Paul Dade, Dick Snyder and 100 others (give or take).

Phil, his wife and children reside in Cincinnati, Ohio – a fact that has in no way changed his lifelong devotion to the Indians, Browns and Cavaliers.

I'd love to hear from you – or connect via social media.
Twitter: @pjbarth
Facebook: Phil Barth
www.philbarth.com
phil@philbarthspeaks.com

Made in the USA
Middletown, DE
31 October 2022

13869592R00102